D1737260

Tired of Living

Studies in Modern European History

Frank J. Coppa
General Editor

Vol. 44

PETER LANG
New York • Washington, D.C./Baltimore • Bern
Frankfurt am Main • Berlin • Brussels • Vienna • Oxford

Ty Geltmaker

Tired of Living

Suicide in Italy
from National Unification
to World War I,
1860–1915

HV
6548
I8
G45
2002

PETER LANG
New York • Washington, D.C./Baltimore • Bern
Frankfurt am Main • Berlin • Brussels • Vienna • Oxford

CALIFORNIA INSTITUTE OF THE ARTS

177142

Library of Congress Cataloging-in-Publication Data

Geltmaker, Ty.
Tired of living: suicide in Italy from national unification
to World War I, 1860–1915 / Ty Geltmaker.
p. cm. — (Studies in modern European history; vol. 44)
Includes bibliographical references and index.
1. Suicide—Italy—History. I. Title: Suicide in Italy from national
unification to World War I, 1860–1915. II. Title. III. Series.
HV6548.I8 G45   362.28'0945—dc21   2001029041
ISBN 0-8204-5544-X
ISSN 0893-6897   9-17-03 dss

Die Deutsche Bibliothek-CIP-Einheitsaufnahme

Geltmaker, Ty:
Tired of living: suicide in Italy from national unification
to World War I, 1860–1915 / Ty Geltmaker.
–New York; Washington, D.C./Baltimore; Bern;
Frankfurt am Main; Berlin; Brussels; Vienna; Oxford: Lang.
(Studies in modern European history; Vol. 44)
ISBN 0-8204-5544-X

The paper in this book meets the guidelines for permanence and durability
of the Committee on Production Guidelines for Book Longevity
of the Council of Library Resources.

© 2002 Peter Lang Publishing, Inc., New York

All rights reserved.
Reprint or reproduction, even partially, in all forms such as microfilm,
xerography, microfiche, microcard, and offset strictly prohibited.

Printed in the United States of America

For James, *mio compagno di vita*,
remembering Echo and Bamboo,
starting over with Ingo,
never tired of living.

Contents

Erratum: Introduction, p. 1:
"Giovanni" Verga, not
"Giuseppe," correctly noted
in notes, bibliography, index.

Acknowledgments

Thanks to the following individuals, even as none was directly involved in the writing of this particular book.

In 1972 Romano Mastromattei, Aldo Rosselli, Diane David, and Tony Lucchesi introduced me to Italian history, literature and art at the Trinity College Rome campus, founded by Michael Campo. With Romano's help I later studied and worked in Perugia, Urbino, and Rome, 1975–79. Thanks also to the assistance of Giorgio Orvieto at the *Università per Stranieri* in Perugia and Jim Long at the *Rome Daily American.*

George Cooper, Frank Kirkpatrick, John Gettier, Borden Painter, and Norman Miller instilled in me a general love of the humanities at Trinity College, Hartford, 1970–74. Borden Painter pioneered the teaching of modern Italian history at Trinity in the 1970s. In New York, Naples, Florence, Scanno, Rome, and Lugano throughout the 1980s my *compagno di vita* James Rosen and I indulged our critical love of all things Italian with Anna Maria Merlino Palermo, Maria Teresa Pacini, Piero Castelli, Susan Rushton, Cristina Bini, Sandro Becucci, and Gitty Darugar. In Rome, 1976–79, Anne Q. Hoy, Cam Mann, Dale McAdoo, and other colleagues at the *Rome Daily American* and *International Daily News*, and my language students at the *Centro di Studi Americani*, *Banca d'Italia*, and *Ministero della Difesa*, helped make sense of my expatriation, as did my colleague Dick Growald at *United Press International* when I left Rome for New York in 1979. Thanks to my Trinity "Rome crowd" of Gail Buxton, David Gellatly, Jim Gayley, and Mark Miller I exiled myself to Rome instead of Berlin. Gianni Cieri-Sciarra and Franco Bartolomei were my best friends in Rome in the 1970s, along with many other *compagni* in the FUORI gay rights group of the *Partito Radicale*. Thanks also to Pierfrancesco Aiello.

My late entry into academia began thanks to a generous fellowship at New York University, 1985–86, where Bert Hansen, Molly Nolan, and Tom Bender plunged me into social and cultural history. When I moved to Los Angeles in 1986, thanks to fellowships at the University of Southern California, Lois Banner, Elinor Accampo, and Rudy Koshar guided me further along the path of studies I had begun at NYU. Margaret Rosenthal made it possible for me to do Italian history at USC, both as a student and teacher. Thanks also at USC to Paul Knoll, Barrie Thorne, Steve Ross, Tom Cox, and Michael Dear.

Victoria de Grazia, Sander Gilman, and Carlo Ginzburg gave invaluable dissertation advice at moments of doubt and crisis. I also thank Dick Hebdige and colleagues and students, especially Craig Stein, at the California Institute of the Arts, 1992–95. Thanks also to all my students at Bronx Community College, 1996–97.

Research for this project was done at the New York Public Library, Rome's National Research Library, Columbia University's Butler Library Paternò Collection, the University of California at Los Angeles Research Library, and the central public libraries of Como, Treviso, Mantua, Ferrara, and Florence. All translations are my own, unless otherwise indicated.

Thanks also to Glyndora Campbell, and Nicholas, Meredith, and Buster; and Vilma and Frances Georgetti, and all other friends in Nyack where I wrote this book. Over more than 20 years Margot Liddell and Benj DeMott have been best critics and friends. Thanks yet again, also, to Milly and Gene Geltmaker, along with Tami, Dede, Danny and Matt. This book is dedicated to James Rosen, remembering our many years of happiness with Echo and Bamboo, now starting over with Ingo, who makes it impossible for us to get tired of living.

Introduction

The sacrifice of our fatherland has been consummated: all is lost; and life, if it can ever be, leaves us to do nothing but weep over our misfortune and our infamy. And we Italians wash our hands in the blood of our own people.
—Ugo Foscolo, *Last Letters of Jacopo Ortis*, 1802

The word Italy *is a geographical expression. Though it is a term that slides easily off the tongue, it has none of the political implications which the revolutionary ideologists are trying to attach to it—implications which would threaten the very existence of the individual states which constitute the Italian peninsula. We are very much concerned over the possible diffusion of these erroneous ideas of nationality.*
—Prince Clemens von Metternich, 1847

I childishly determined to dress always in black, fancying myself in mourning for my country. Jacopo Ortis *happened to fall into my hands at this time, and the reading of it became a passion with me. I learned it by heart. Matters went so far that my poor mother became terrified lest I should commit suicide.*
—Giuseppe Mazzini, 1864

This book is a brief social, cultural, and intellectual history of suicide in Italy from 1860–61 to 1915. These dates correspond to Italy's national unification and emergence as a world power and modern state. In suicide, as in other areas of national development, Italy in this period was rapidly "catching up" with its more industrially advanced neighbors.

As all students of Italian history know, the patriotic writings of Mazzini, coupled with the military moves of Garibaldi and the diplomatic maneuvers of Cavour—along with the sacrifices of thousands of individual citizens—made the promised legend of a united Italian peninsula a reality repeatedly still waiting to be fully realized.

Over the course of 1860–61 Garibaldi and his troops won over most of Italy south of Rome from the Spanish Bourbons who for centuries had controlled Naples and the territories stretching south to Sicily. As the contemporary Sicilian writer Giuseppe Verga made clear, many people in these territories south of Rome did not necessarily care much that they had been "liberated" from their former rulers, as they soon learned they had become subjects of a French-speaking royal family from the distant north.[1] The Savoia dynasty was undeterred, piecing together a new Italy from its holdings in Piedmont, with a capital at Turin, and the island of Sardinia and the new holdings south of Rome. At this moment the Vatican still controlled Rome and central Italy, and Austria still held Venice and its territories. Piedmont had gained Lombardy and Milan in 1859. In 1866, Venice and some but not all of the Hapsburg lands of "unredeemed" Italy fell to the champions of *Italia irredenta*. The fall of Rome as a French protectorate under fragile Vatican control on September 20, 1870 sealed the deal. It could no longer be said that Italy was just "a geographical expression." A half century later, in May 1915, hoping to gain the last of its "unredeemed" lands in the north and east, Italy entered World War I—renouncing its treaties with Germany and the Austro-Hungarian Empire—on the side of England and France. The following history of suicide in this political context, and in an era of unparalleled social and economic change, is intimately connected to related questions and uncertainties in this period over what it meant to be Italian and what was the role of the Italian state both on the world stage and in the daily life of its citizens.

Since this story of suicide in this time and place has never before been told, it is narrated here as a simple tale, even if elaborately footnoted.[2] The extensive documentation should free the reader to follow the basic narrative: From the moment Italy became a unified modern nation it was riven by a real epidemic of suicide and preoccupied with a national debate over why so many citizens of the new country were killing themselves. The suicide epidemic seemed to stop only when the country went to war, with only more deaths piling one on top of the other, this time however in the name of patriotic love.

This terse tale should free other historians to use the data and narratives provided here for further analysis and investigation of this topic and related issues. This is just the first version of a story here first told, deliberately bled of every possible reference to current or recent theoretical perspectives, which might bear some fruit in future analyses. This is only the story of what happened then and there: Many Italians were killing themselves over the turn of the century, and many more Italians were worried and were wondering why.

Among the many explanations for the wave of suicide in this period most commentators agreed that the trend was a "necessary safety valve" peculiar to Italy's late political and economic development. Popular "degeneration" theories added scientific credibility to such psychological and sociological analyses, many of which focused on supposed erotic components to the act of suicide itself. The Vatican, for its part, linked the publicized rise in suicide—which was also partly the result of improved statistical gathering of the ascendant state—to the establishment of the abhorred secular, unified nation itself. Many critics also pointed to the literary depiction of suicide as having a hypnotic effect on susceptible individuals. Meanwhile, contemporary commentators viewed a resurgence of dueling and a fascination with war as symptoms of degeneracy in a society increasingly subject to the many forms of "indirect suicide," not unlike current American understandings of so-called "suicide by cop."

This study of suicide is just one expanded part of a larger study of honor and national identity in Italy at the turn of the twentieth century. It evolved, was written, and then shortened as a separate study after having found the evidence herein presented while researching newspaper reporting of the mock violence of the famed *Serate futuriste* (Futurist Evenings) across northern Italy from 1909–1915.

Despite my stated disinterest in theorizing this tale too much at this point, I want to suggest that the story I am about to tell offers some evidence that the French theorist Rene Girard was onto something when he remarked: "Sacrifice is the most crucial and fundamental of rites."[3] I accept, as the result of research well beyond the boundaries of this study, Girard's hypothesis that violence is trans-historically endemic to most, if not all, societies, even as I am most interested in identifying historically specific sites, times and conditions of particular acts of violence and their representations.

By way of some examples culled from my research of violence in modern Italy I want to suggest that the illogical, confusing web of cultural cohesion which Girard has described as an underlying, endemic system of social rivalry between the envious imitator and the flattered, but threatened, imitated— "the mechanism of mimetic desire"—is also an erotic joust or duel, which sometimes masquerades itself as suicide or war. In this respect the relationship of sport and violence as discussed by contemporary critics such as Mario Morasso are linked to later writings on the nature of play by Johan Huizinga, as well as to Norman O. Brown's assertion: "The aim of Eros is union with objects outside the self; and at the same time Eros is fundamentally narcissistic, self-loving."[4]

I would suggest even further that Girard's understanding of endemic, uncontrolled killing and mob violence, as being brought under control and rationalized through ritual sacrifices of surrogate victims, is not limited to the sacred world of religion, especially at a moment in history when the state eclipses the church as the literal and mythic altar on which controlled, redemptive sacrifice is carried out.

In the five chapters of this modest book, the first chapter deals with press reports and psychosexual analyses of the ever more shocking number of suicides rattling the new Italian nation. A more sober, sociological overview and consideration of complex statistical issues is dealt with in chapter two. The underlying hostility between religious and secular forces, especially with regard to suicide, is the subject of chapter three. Chapter four takes the contemporary cultural and legal debate over issues of life and death backward in time, especially in terms of suicide and historical questions about martyrdom and the role of literature in influencing people to kill themselves. Chapter five examines what contemporary critics called "indirect suicide," in the context of a resurgent popularity of the duel and rabble rousing for war. Suicide is at once the focus of this study and the lens through which this period of Italian national identity formation is examined. It will occasionally be the case that what is not said is highlighted to be as important as what was said, especially with regard to taboo topics such as homosexuality, which in this period were only beginning to be tentatively addressed.

Notes

[1] Giovanni Verga, *Novelle rusticane* (Milan, 1883; English transl. by D.H. Lawrence, 1925, *Little Novels of Sicily,* New York: Grove Press, 1953, repr. South Royalton: Steerforth Italia, 2000).

[2] Recent valuable studies concerning suicide do not cover the story herein told. See George Minois, *History of Suicide:Voluntary Death in Western Culture* (Johns Hopkins University Press, 1999; orig. *Histoire du suicide: La société occidentale face à la morte volontaire,* Paris: Librarie Arthème Fayard, 1995) for a broad and detailed overview with scant attention (p. 274, p. 300) given to modern Italy; and Thomas Harrison, *1910: The Emancipation of Desire* (Berkeley: University of California Press, 1996) for emphasis on the suicidal figure of Carlo Michelstaedter in the context of Trieste/Austro-Hungarian fin-de-siècle culture.

[3] Rene Girard, *Violence and the Sacred* (Batimore: Johns Hopkins University Press, 1977; orig. *La violence et le sacré:* Paris, 1972), cited in Walter Burkert, Rene Girard, and Jonathan Z. Smith, *Violent Origins: Ritual Killing and Cultural Formation* (Stanford: Stanford University Press, 1987), p. 7.

[4] Johan Huizinga, *Homo Ludens: A Study of the Play Element in Culture* (Boston: Beacon Press, 1955; orig. Leyden, 1938); Norman O. Brown, *Life Against Death: The Psychoanalytical Meaning of History* (Middletown: Wesleyan University Press, 1959), p. 45.

1. A Necessary Epidemic

A review of the Italian press in the half-century from national unification to World War I reveals increasing public concern over a growing number of suicides and suicide attempts. As one later critic observed in a study of the work of Siena's end-of-century, "pessimist" writer Federigo Tozzi,

> Browsing through the newspapers that circulated in Siena during Tozzi's youth, one discovers that the city was active above all else in the insanity of suicide. It is impossible to estimate how many Sienese—whose population was about 25,000— caught between living and dying, voluntarily took the second route.[1]

A young Sienese girl breaks a few plates and throws herself out of a fifth-story window; a laundress drinks a deadly solution of mercuric chloride; a hunchback sets himself on fire; a cobbler drowns himself by jumping into a well and a woman tosses her body weighted by roped rocks into a stream; a man slashes his wrists while sitting at the kitchen sink; an old woman and two farmers hang themselves together; and a mechanic jumps to his death from a window, only to be followed by his neighbor, the tailor. These Sienese cases are typical of suicide reports from the regional press of the period, especially in the northern half of the new nation.

By 1910 the problem was so acute in Milan that a *sala dei tentati suicidi* was established at the city's *Ospedale Maggiore*. The existence of such an officially designated "recovery room for attempted suicides," as well as voluminous press reports of unsuccessful suicide attempts, suggests that the number of Italians who were apparently trying to kill themselves was indeed great, and that many who tried were either inept or ambivalent at the moment of their attempted self destruction. Typical of those suicidal Milanese citizens who survived to be admitted to the hospital's designated facility was one 27-year-old Silvio Astolfoni. When asked what had led him to swallow a solution of mercuric chloride, the distraught young man replied: "*Ero stanco di vivere*," that he was "tired of living."[2]

In the same years, in Florence, suicide jumps from the bridges and embankments of the Arno were commonly reported in the local press. In one such attempt on a late September night in 1913, a 25-year-old male landed alive but stranded in shallow waters and thick mud only to be rescued by night watchmen in sculls commandeered from the adjacent boathouse of the *Libertas* rowing club.[3]

In the provincial cities, too, the problem seemed out of control. What, for example, led 15 year-old Ines Botti of via Garibaldi in Ferrara to swallow a potion of tincture of iodine and sulfuric acid just after three o'clock on the afternoon of March 23, 1911? Both her family and her boyfriend discounted *"disgusto col'innamorato,"* or loathing for said boyfriend himself as the cause of young Ines' unsuccessful attempt to end her life. While expressing relief at the girl's resuscitation, the *Gazzetta Ferrarese* editorialized:

> This mania of young people to throw themselves into death's arms is a true symptom of our race's degeneracy; these youths, as in this case, have experienced little or nothing of life and its affairs, so that they ought to take life still on its best terms, considering their age; why are there now so many young people who no longer feel that instinct of self-survival which is so natural and overwhelming even in the most wretched categories of animals?

The unsigned editorial ends in despair, lamenting: "Inexplicable mystery, moral anomaly!"[4]

Among his many investigations of this wave of suicides which baffled editorialists, the contemporary social psychologist Enrico Altavilla cited the 1906 Bologna case of one 14-year-old Alfredo Ragni, who early one November morning hanged himself in an upstairs storage room while at work in the popular Rovinazzi pastry shop. Minutes earlier the young Ragni, known for his "jovial humor," had jokingly asked an unsuspecting co-worker if the twine he held "would be enough to hang a man," adding: "If I'm not back soon it's no big deal, it just means I hanged myself."[5]

Altavilla explains the apparently happy youth's self-destructive act as stemming not from any "nervous exhaustion" or "external factor" but rather from a simple "desire to shock his friends with eccentric behavior."[6] Citing the French sociologist Louis Proal's 1907 study *L'education et le suicide des enfants* as his authority on this matter, Altavilla argued:

> Suicide among young people is more frequent than commonly believed, because being less thoughtful but strongly sensitive, they lack a grown-up fear of death, to which they are often drawn by a momentary impulse caused by something minor such as a scolding or a disappointment.[7]

With regard to eccentricity, Altavilla's reasoning was in line with the contemporary German sociologist Georg Simmel's 1903 essay *"The Metropolis and Mental Life."*[8] For Simmel, modern individuals were psychologically re-fitting themselves, erecting new "metropolitan individualities" in order to cope with the "intensification of emotional life due to the swift and continuous shift of external and internal stimuli." Unleashed from traditional restraints on one's behavior and constraining but verifying assurances of one's social place and value, the modern individual, according to Simmel, became preoccupied with "giving one's own personality a certain status." Simmel notes:

> Where quantitative increase of value and energy has reached its limits, one seizes on qualitative distinctions, so that, through taking advantage of existing sensitivity to differences, the attention of the social world can, in some way, be won for oneself.[9]

Without linking this self-assertive tendency to any particular behavior, suicidal or not, Simmel simply states:

> This leads ultimately to the strangest eccentricities, to specifically metropolitan extravagances of self-distanciation, of caprice, of fastidiousness, the meaning of which is no longer to be found in the content of such activity itself but rather in its being a form of 'being different'—of making oneself noticeable.[10]

This 20th-century psychological condition, which fused indifference with eccentricity was nothing new for readers of the popular nineteenth-century French author Honoré de Balzac, who, writing of his capital city in 1833, argued at some deservedly quotable length:

> The Parisian is interested in everything and nothing. No dominant emotion has left its mark on his countenance over which so many emotions have skimmed, and therefore it turns grey, like the plaster of the house-fronts, overlaid with all shades of dust and smoke. Truth to tell, the Parisian, caring for nothing one day for what will delight him the day after, lives like a child whatever his age may be.

> He grumbles at everything and puts up with everything, mocks at everything, forgets and longs for everything, likes to sample everything; he passionately takes up a cause and drops it without a further thought—royalism, foreign conquest, national glory, any idol be it of bronze or tinsel. He sheds them as he sheds his hose, hats, or dreams of fortune.

> In Paris no sentiment can stand against the swirling torrent of events; their onrush and the effort to swim against the current lessens the intensity of passion. Love is

reduced to desire, hate to a whimsy. The only family link is with the thousand-franc note; one's only friend is the pawnbroker.

This general attitude of devil-may-care bears its fruit: in the salon as in the street no one is *de trop*, no one is absolutely indispensable or absolutely noxious, be he knave or blockhead, intelligent man or honest citizen.

In Paris there is toleration for everything: the government, the guillotine, the Church, cholera.

In a hauntingly sarcastic conclusion to his backhanded paean to modern French life, sixty years before the Italians began to organize themselves into a nation-state of similar ambitions, Balzac warns:

You will always be welcome in Parisian society, but if you are not there no one will miss you.[11]

Besides speculating on already established European explanations of eccentric behavior, most of which did not address the contemporary suicide phenomenon, Altavilla also recorded numerous cases of boys and men who in search of a higher sexual pleasure and psychic awareness, hanged themselves in the act of orgasmic auto-asphyxia. Citing an unidentified text by the contemporary Italian criminologist Cesare Lombroso, Altavilla describes one such incident in which a 50-year-old man hanged himself to full public view in his window, leaving a suicide note saying he was very happy and just wanted to experience an ecstatic sexual pleasure he had read about in a medical dictionary. The suicide note ends with the oddly felicitous admonition:

Don't anyone cry for me; instead, all of you should say: There's a man who has known every human happiness.[12]

The forensic anthropologist Enrico Ferri cited a related incident a few years earlier in which a retarded 20-year-old boy accepted the paid dare of two male acquaintances to hang himself so they could observe the anticipated physiological effects of his mixed pleasure and agony. After accepting the offered fee of 70 *centesimi* for ten minutes of torture, the unfortunate youth managed to survive, twisting and turning for five minutes before going into spasms. Panicked, the paying audience of two let go of the rope from which the object of their entertainment was appended, leaving him to "fall to ground, deprived of all senses." At a judicial hearing the defendants were assigned minimal fines after it was argued that they were "only having fun," as evidenced by the lack of permanent injuries to their willing victim.[13]

While noting that "for a long time it has been believed that hanging was accompanied by erection and orgasm" (*"spasmo venereo"*), Altavilla cites countervailing contemporary medical studies which claimed to show that post-mortem physical evidence of such alleged orgasms were in fact the result of "putrefaction or circulatory stagnation caused by prolonged suspension, along with paralysis of the seminal vesicle sphincters."[14]

Despite these medical arguments that practitioners of this suicidal ritual did not in fact experience an erotic pleasure, Altavilla refers to related cases in the professional literature of the period, describing men becoming obsessively preoccupied with hanging, genital erection, and orgasm, incapable of sexual arousal without applying potentially fatal pressure to their own throats. In one such case, a building superintendent was reported to have overheard details of such a suicide, leading him to a three-year "erotic-suicidal obsession" consisting of "impulsive urges to copulate" accompanied by "a lustful desire to squeeze his neck to the point of strangulation."[15]

In his attempt to explain this male erotic-suicidal behavior Altavilla mentions the character Jacques Lantier as portrayed in Emile Zola's 1890 novel *La Bête Humaine.* Zola had been greatly influenced by Lombroso's theories on crime and aberrant behavior, popularly disseminated under the general concept that there existed a class of "born criminals" whose atavistic behaviors represented a "degeneration" back to a primitive barbarism which occasionally re-emerged to challenge the norms of modern society.

The proclivity to commit crimes and engage in abnormal activities could, it was thought, be anthropometrically gauged through analysis of photographs, interpretations of tattoos, and measurement of body parts of both the living and the dead. Such human specimens, consisting mainly of inmates of state prisons and asylums to which Lombroso had access as a government physician, were routinely diagnosed with any number of innately degenerative conditions, the most common of which was a vaguely-defined, generic "epilepsy." Lombroso's laboratory contained scores of human skulls, skeletons, and preserved heads, as well as art, pottery, and other craftwork made by institutionalized "degenerates."[16]

Lombroso further argued that there was an organic relationship between progress and degenerate activity, such that in all modern societies a significant sub-population of "men of genius" shared some of the non-conformist traits found in the "born criminal."[17] In *Genio e degenerazione* (*Genius and Degeneration*) Lombroso asserted:

> The most paradoxical aspect of my theory of genius, the basis of which is psychopathological and degenerative, is singularly confirmed by observing the analagous process in natural evolution wherein every progress is grafted onto a regression and every evolutionary movement is based on a regressive movement.[18]

Such vague theories linking social progress and cultural decline may at first glance seem tied to popular simplifications of Charles Darwin's contemporary observations on evolution. In fact, however, Lombroso's views were more closely related to the contemporary German biologist Ernst Haeckel's theory of "recapitulation," which stated: "Ontogeny recapitulates phylogeny." Haeckle, who was widely read by Italian naturalists and forensic researchers, argued that the development from conception to death of the individual biological unit follows, or "recapitulates," in parallel phases, the evolutionary development of the biological group to which that individual belongs.

But, according to Haeckle, not all individual biological units reach the fully developed stage of their group's most evolutionarily advanced members. Some individuals and some whole sub-groups grow even into old age, it was argued, retaining incompletely developed infantile or juvenile traits. This condition of arrested evolutionary development, or incomplete growth out of the process of "recapitulation," was known as "paedomorphosis." The actual process of this alleged developmental retardation was known as "neotony." In Lombroso's work these two unwieldy terms are replaced with the more accessible "atavism," referring to once common primitive traits, which "resurface" long after they have generally gone out of circulation.

Such obscurantist theorizing provided an apparently scientific explanation for alleged physical and intellectual inferiorities among whole human groups, especially women and non-whites, while also explaining the assumed monopoly on genius among some white males. It should be noted that Darwin explicitly rejected Haeckel's formulations.[19]

Applying this scientific theory to human society, Lombroso believed a social minority of "men of genius" and "born criminals" shared a "love of the new" and engaged in abnormal behavior because of an uncontrolled "excess of intelligence compensated for by a lack of moral sense and practical energy."[20]   Thus, Lombroso notes: "The list of suicides of great genius is enormous."   He cites a litany of famous intellectuals and artists who killed themselves and also quotes statistical figures from studies by the contemporary suicidologist Enrico Morselli, alleging to show that suicide rates in Italy were highest among literary men (619 per million inhabitants) and professors (355 per million), and lowest among unskilled workers (36 per million) and priests (53 per million). As will be clear in later coverage of Morselli's statistical study of suicide (Ch. 2), the raw number of suicides among the agricultural and working classes by far outdistanced suicides among the well-educated, minority elite.[21]

In *Genio e degenerazione* and among the more than sixty titles published in the prestigious *Biblioteca antropologico-giuridica* series, Lombroso and his colleagues studied the "atavistic" personalities of Italian literary heroes such as Alessandro Manzoni, Vittorio Alfieri and Giacomo Leopardi alongside common criminals and other degenerates.[22]

In this context of degeneration theory and with reference to Zola's literary invention in the appropriately titled *Human Beast*, Altavilla suggests that male erotic-suicide lies at the most masochistic extreme of a spectrum of abnormal, atavistic behaviors whose most opposite, sadistic extreme consists of male murder of the female sexual partner during orgasm. Altavilla asserts:

> We know sadism finds its most ferocious expression in the need to murder the female partner, mixing sexual orgasm with spasms of agony. Emile Zola immortalized the character Jacques Lantier, who could not even dream of sensual intoxication without associating it with the desperate need to kill. So, I ask myself: Could the opposite degeneration—masochism—reach such an extreme that love and death infuse each other in a single sentiment of lust?[23]

Altavilla further argues that this "death wish" as it relates to male sexual activity is based not just in the anatomical physiology of ejaculation, but also in the different zoological functions of the male and the female in the perpetuation of the species. Women, according to Altavilla, rarely connect sexual activity and such a death wish because "the female who copulates is just beginning, not exhausting her sexual function," which is to carry a child to birth, thus preserving both herself and the species. Men, however, whose sexually zoological function stops, according to Altavilla, with "the emission of the seed," are for this very reason more likely to link orgasm with death. Without saying so, Altavilla invokes here the ancient understanding of male sexual ejaculation as a "little death," which prompted the third-century Christian writer Tertullian to wonder:

> I cannot help asking, whether we do not, in that very heat of extreme gratification when the generative fluid is ejected, feel that some of our soul is gone out from us?[24]

Instead, Altavilla introduces the ostensibly more scientific, supporting examples of certain butterfly, praying mantis, and other insect reproduction groups, whereby, among bees, for example:

> At the exact moment in which the only queen takes off in her nuptial flight, all the males take off to chase her. Just one fortunate male, the quickest and strongest, manages to reach her. In the elation of copulating this male abandons all his genital organs in the body of the female and he dies.[25]

In further elucidation of the psychosexual understanding of suicide with regard to male and female behavior during this period of Italian life, Altavilla cites an unattributed commentary contained in an undated news article printed in the authoritative Milan daily *Il Corriere della Sera*. The case concerns the suicide death of a teen-aged girl, and after noting that "To be fifteen and to be good-looking are two reasons to be happy for a woman," the writer notes:

> But then, to kill yourself is in itself astonishing. But it is even more astonishing to kill yourself in front of a mirror, wanting to see yourself, your pretty face and your delicate white throat, in the act of inflicting your own death; to keep your eyes open and unblinking in the exact moment in which the splash of blood drowns and butchers the living visions accrued in just fifteen years, and to face death in a mirror in order to feel it as an intimate experience which a romantic person would call sublime, is in reality to have committed a double suicide.[26]

Altavilla disagrees with this analysis, which he says is "very nice," but argues instead:

It was not the impression of a double suicide that the young woman in front of the mirror wanted to give; but no, she wished to make her suicide seem like a homicide.[27]

Emphasizing his assertion that the young girl wanted to make it "seem" as if she were being murdered, Altavilla claims this suicide was an attempt to experience one's own bloody death as a masturbatory substitute for a double suicide or for murder at the hands of an amorous accomplice. Without giving further information regarding this young girl's sexual history, Altavilla uses the parlance of the day to explain her suicide as an act of lesbian masturbation:

For sexual degenerates, suicide is in fact the funereal equivalent of masturbation, by which such people adapt to the impossibility of ever finding anyone who could satisfy their abnormal instincts.[28]

Without using the then novel but increasingly popular term "homosexual," Altavilla employs the vocabulary of degeneracy theory to imply that a case of same-sex desire or fantasy led to the young girl's slashing suicide. Terms such as "sexual perversion," "sexual degeneracy," "degenerate," and the even more explicit "sexual inversion," or "invert," while potentially inclusive of all sexual behaviors not rigidly defined as properly pro-creative, referred in contemporary clinical language and in common speech specifically to erotic activity, imagined or real, between members of the same sex.[29]

Curiously, Altavilla did not proffer similarly plausible explanations of squelched same-sex desire or repressed homoerotic yearnings as a cause of suicide among those males who killed themselves while committing the allegedly overtly erotic act of orgasmic auto-asphyxia. Altavilla's reference in this case to "the impossibility of ever finding anyone who could satisfy their abnormal instincts" is doubly curious since Italy had for centuries been identified as a Mediterranean haven—often against all climatological and officially acknowledged cultural reality—for northerners in need of sunshine and same-sex romance. The very word "*Florenzer*" was, since Renaissance times, a German noun meaning "sodomite."[30]

More intriguing still is the fact that in 1889—two decades before Altavilla's condemnatory pronouncement on the subject—the Italian parliament decriminalized all sexual relations between any and all individuals of either sex above the age of twelve. The relevant statute does not even mention same-sex relations.[31] Decriminalization did not, however, mean that homosexuality was culturally accepted. As the jurist Giulio Crivellari noted in his exhaustive study of united Italy's first unitary penal code, this law "says nothing about un-natural libidinous acts" except if they are committed by force, with under-aged persons, or in public places.[32] In fact, Italian newspapers of the period regularly reported the arrest of individuals charged with having committed euphemistically defined "*atti sconci*," or "lewd behavior."[33]

Lombroso himself advocated the decriminalization of certain same-sex sexual behaviors even as he continued to regard such activity as un-natural and, in some cases, worthy of incarceration. The 1911 English edition of Lombroso's constantly revised *L'uomo delinquente*, published as *Crime: Its Causes and Remedies,* leaves no doubt about his position with regard to homosexuality.

> Homo-sexual offenders whose crime has been occasioned by residence in barracks, or colleges, or by a forced celibacy, plainly will not relapse when the cause has been removed. It will be sufficient in their case to inflict a conditional punishment, for they are not to be confused with the homo-sexual offenders who are born such, and who manifest their evil propensities from childhood without being determined by special causes.

Lombroso's forgiving approach to momentary lapses in conforming to the strict codes of heterosexual behavior was countered with a severe policy of social containment and ostracization toward inveterate degenerates.

> These born homo-sexuals should be confined from their youth, for they are a source of contagion and cause a great number of occasional criminals.[34]

Such a clear division between types of individuals engaged for allegedly different reasons in the same illicit homosexual behavior was also linked with popular understandings of the bi-polar duality of male and female gender identity. Criminality and homosexuality were located at the crossroads of gender "inversion." In this sense, Lombroso asserted:

> The influence of degeneration always tends to meld and blend the sexes, so that among male criminals one finds a feminine childishness, which leads to pederasty, corresponding to a masculinity among female criminals indicating an atavistic return to the hermaphroditic period.[35]

This schematic understanding of the place of sexual identity and criminal behavior in the process of degeneration was also useful in explaining sacred ritual and spirituality. Priests and holy men, according to Lombroso, wear vestments traditionally identified with female clothing in order to distinguish themselves and their atavistic, spiritually hypnotic functions from the secular, militarily-influenced, more modern male wardrobe. This identification of the female with the more primitive atavistic experience is, for Lombroso, "easily explainable."

> Women more easily become hysterical, they are also inclined to become hypnotic, giving rise to truly mysterious phenomena such as telepathy and communicating with spirits.[36]

Within the parameters of these clinical definitions, Lombroso analyzed the renowned early-nineteenth-century Italian author Giacomo Leopardi. The great north-central Italian poet's early melancholy life, defined by constant conflict with his parents, and his later homosexual relationship in Naples with the younger Antonio Ranieri were commonly known facts in their day. For Lombroso, however, what mattered with regard to Leopardi and his recognized talent was the link between the esteemed poet's genius and his innate but reviled identity as a sexual degenerate:

> It is well known how he became a hunchback because of his abusive masturbation since his most tender years, and how this was part and parcel of his literary precociousness.[37]

The contemporary critic Scipio Sighele, who was primarily concerned with the ways in which literature influenced and suggestively induced individuals to engage in degenerate and criminal behavior, including suicide, shared Lombroso's revulsion of same-sex sexual relations and behavior. In his criticisms of D'Annunzio's *L'Innocente*, Flaubert's *Madame Bovary*, Zola's *La Bête Humaine*, Eugène Sue's *Les Mystères de Paris*, and George Sand's *Indiana*, among other notable works, Sighele condemned infanticide, adultery, and all manner of degenerate behavior, reserving special disapproval for same-sex eroticism.

Giving his greatest attention to "criminal couples," in literature and in real life, Sighele condemns the "*coppia tribade*" and the "*coppia cineda*" as the lowest possible arrangement of human life. These so-called Tribadists (derived from the Greek verb "to rub") and the Cinedas (derived from ancient Mediterranean slang for "prostitute") were those men and women who had sexual relations with people of their own allegedly "third" sex. After having analyzed crimes committed by heterosexuals, Sighele invites his readers to "descend even deeper, despite the revulsion one can feel, into these underground societies."

> Let's wade into this muck which has by now even come to the surface. Here we will find degenerate couples bonded no longer by love, but by a monstrous parody of this sentiment.[38]

Sighele criticzes homosexual relations as "the strangest, the most abject, and fortunately, the rarest of unions that can tie two individuals together."[39] Lesbian relationships are oddly caught in Sighele's condemnatory web. On the one hand they are defined as being abnormal; at the same time they are characterized as a mimicry of heterosexual love. "*I rapporti lesbici*," or lesbian relationships, Sighele asserts, "are born and maintain themselves, as happens in normal love, under the force of seduction by one of the 'tribadists' on the other."[40]

Except for Altavilla's earlier analysis of the sexually degenerate causes of the suicide of the teen-aged girl who slit her throat in front of a mirror, none of these other dissections of same-sex degeneracy linked such conditions to suicide. And this is for a good reason, since even Altavilla argued that the girl in his example actually wanted to make it seem as if she had been murdered by an amorous accomplice. In fact, all of these contemporary interpreters of modern Italian life classified same-sex degeneracy as an atavistic condition of arrested evolutionary development. As such, homosexuality was associated with other atavistic conditions and practices representing resurgent traits of primitive barbarism.

Within this scheme, all types of violence were ranked evolutionarily across a range of destructive behaviors. Homicide and same-sex sexual relations were ranked at the primitive, atavistic end of this spectrum. Thus, homosexuality and murder were identified as stemming from similar if not identical stages of arrested evolutionary development. However much the taking of one's own life may have been deplored, under this formula suicide, even though it was also identified with hyper-sensitive homosexuality, was ranked with heterosexuality at the opposite, civilized extreme of the developmental scale.

Exact ratios of numbers of homicides compared to suicides were gathered and illustrated in charts and graphs in order to prove, as the contemporary researcher Enrico Ferri put it, "that there is a verifiable antagonism of respective frequency between homicide and suicide."[41] According to these statistics and charts, homicide decreased and suicide increased with social and economic progress.

This alleged inverse relationship between atavistic homicide and "civilizing" suicide means that during this period of Italian life homosexuality, and murder, despite the decriminalization of the former, were ranked on an equally degenerative footing. Suicide, on the other hand, was not only not considered to be one possible result of the repression of socially proscribed, if privately legal, homoerotic activity, but was ironically viewed as being a regrettable indicator of cultural progress.

However contradictory this formulation may now seem, it allowed contemporary social observers a conceptual framework in which genius, homosexuality, and suicide could be explained away without confronting the possibility that the repression of "un-natural" sexual "inversion" might be a major cause of suicide. Instead, atavistic, degenerative conditions which in the common criminal or in distant, lesser-evolved human societies would have led to murder, were thought in the modern era to lead to suicide. It should be noted that this Italian approach was not universally accepted. For all he held in common with his Italian contemporaries, the German sexologist Richard von Krafft-Ebbing did suggest suicide in this period was unusually common among sexual "inverts" afraid of being blackmailed or shamefully revealed to a scornful public.[42]

It should be further noted that Altavilla, Ferri, and Lombroso were convinced that degeneracy theory was a scientific step forward, away from rigid, impersonal legal categories which were thought to have more in common with ecclesiastical moralism than with modern science. Ferri succinctly criticized those who "in the classical tradition continue to consider the crime (an abstraction) rather than the criminal (a real living person) as we of the 'positivist' school advocate."[43] Even early homosexual rights advocates such as Karl Ulrichs and other activist reformers in contemporary Germany and England accepted this "positivist" emphasis on categorizing human types rather than criminalizing certain behavior, to the point that they themselves embraced the taxonomic language of "sexual inversion" theory while rejecting the Italian "degenerative" corollary.[44]

Among his many other analyses, Altavilla also suggested both religious and physiological connections between modern suicide and Christian traditions of self-abnegation, mortification of the flesh, and martyrology. This relationship was most vividly asserted in Altavilla's bold pronouncement:

> Christ came to die for mankind, and so essentially was a suicide.[45]

The flagellant tradition, which enjoyed an especially popular following in practice and in art throughout Italy in the twelfth and thirteenth centuries, is directly related to modern suicide, especially by hanging, according to Altavilla. Citing a seventeenth-century Italian medical treatise on the subject, Altavilla notes: "The aphrodisiacal effect of flagellation has been known since the most ancient of times."[46]

Altavilla further asserts that from a physiological point of view modern suicide by hanging is "a perversion identical to that of the flagellants."

> Given that the nerves responsible for sexual lust emanate from the lumbar plexus, the spinal cord, with its close connection, can have a reflex excitation on those nerves, all of which is demonstrated by the fact that the act of flagellation usually covers the entire spinal cord, becoming more intense in the lumbar region. Since hanging substitutes pressure for lashing, and a continuous excitement in place of an intermittent one, the phenomenon is essentially the same.[47]

By the end of his study of suicide, Altavilla had categorized and built a hierarchy of every possible psychological motive for the taking of one's own life. The death of a lover, for example, was allegedly a more common cause of suicide among women than among men because, according to Altavilla, "as Madame de Stael has noted, for the male love is an anecdote, an episode, while for the poor woman love is a serious event, a whole history."[48] Futhermore, Altavilla argues that there is a social reason for allegedly higher rates of suicide among betrayed females than among cuckolded males, namely "the strange assumption that the man is responsible for the honor of the woman and that he must be the avenger of it." Altavilla continues:

> While a betrayed wife who commits suicide is always the object of compassion, a husband who sought such drastic escape from his pain would seem to most people to be simply ridiculous.[49]

Lombroso cited similar reasons for female suicide in the wake of failed or betrayed love:

> Abandonment by her lover does not rouse a feeling for revenge because she experiences this as if it were his death, causing such anguish that without him her only consolation is either to kill herself or go insane.[50]

The reverse of this ostensibly compassionate view of the aggrieved, suicidal woman was reserved for the woman who, instead of taking her own life took the life of another, especially within her own family. In a front-page newspaper article titled *"Between the Old and the New: Immoral Pity,"* detailing the strangling of a young girl by her mother in Ferrara in the spring of 1911, an un-named local reporter cites the opinion of the writer Ada Negri:

> A deviant woman is capable of much greater malice than is a man; in women one finds both the highest peaks of idealism and the lowest levels of deprivation. Just think of a woman who abuses her child. A man cannot compete with a woman on this criminal level since aside from all else, a father is not a mother.[51]

This common understanding of the presumably different emotional investment of women and men in affectional life was given scientific credibility as observed and verifiable fact in the many craniometric, photographic, and other body-part measurement studies conducted by Lombroso and his colleagues, including his daughter, on hundreds of arrested female prostitutes and criminals.[52]

Such physiognomically measured assumptions of physiologically defined female moral superiority and rational inferiority, leading to expectations that women would be honored as long as they tolerated all manner of discomfort and abuse, were written into Italian law. Even the 1889 liberal revision of the national penal code provided that a wife found guilty of adultery could be jailed from three to thirty months, while a husband proven to have committed the same offense could be found guilty and punished with the same span of jail time only if he had "kept a concubine in the conjugal house, or notoriously elsewhere."

Further reflecting such disparities, the male lover of a married woman could be jailed for up to thirty months, while the female lover of a married man—presumably his kept possession, and not even worthy of a respectable jail term—could receive a maximum one-year sentence.[53] Under this glaring legal disparity Altavilla's comment on the laughableness of a married man killing himself over his wife's infidelity makes perfect sense.

And sexual life, as defined by Altavilla, Lombroso, and other clinical investigators of the period, can certainly not have meant the same thing to women and to men in a period when even progressive legal statutes continued to define rape as an offense against "good behavior and family order," rather than as a life-threatening attack on a single individual.[54] It should be noted, however, that Lombroso argued against criminal penalties for adultery, instead advocating civil divorce and property settlements.[55] And with regard to the female criminality, which he so assiduously studied, Lombroso noted "an extraordinary increase" in recent years, which he interpreted as yet another "paradoxical sign of civilization's very progress."[56] Lombroso's argument here is not that it was good that women were committing more crime, or that it was proper that women were increasingly involved in public life beyond the confines of domestic isolation, but rather that as more women did emerge from traditional roles, entering into a male-identified public sphere, it was only natural that more crime would be committed by them, as they acted more and more like men.

As the previously cited journalistic reports and anecdotes indicate, any number of timeless reasons and personal crises led Italians, no differently than any other individuals throughout history, to attempt to kill themselves for personal reasons of sadness or despair or fantasy at the turn of the nineteenth century. However fantastical their reasonings may seem now, Italian researchers like Altavilla, Lombroso, and Ferri sought to place these personal stories in what they thought to be enlightened psychosexual and evolutionary perspective.

But in the end, Altavilla's psychological analysis explains everything at once and nothing in particular. Altavilla himself argued:

> Every feeling, degenerating into a morbid state of passion, can be the cause of suicide; but among these love ranks first.[57]

Love, for Altavilla, however, is less an emotion or a sentimental state than it is a dangerous turf mined with destructive potential. He asks himself "if love is a physiological or pathological state," answering:

> Here I will only say that love always represents a profound disruption of the human personality, a period in which almost every organic activity increases such

that the individual acquires an unusual impulsiveness, often a violent reaction to every painful stimulus.[58]

Such painful stimuli, by Altavilla's own analysis, need not be confined to the vicissitudes and stress of personal life in the most narrowly defined psychological categories of the new century. Expanding on earlier, nineteenth-century studies of suicide, which had established the groundwork for his own psychological investigations, Altavilla willingly noted:

> As we have seen elsewhere, suicide degenerates occasionally from an episodic degenerate act into an epidemic; this happens in periods of transition between two civilizations, two faiths, two economic orders. This explains the extraordinary number of suicides in our current epoch; we find ourselves in a neutral zone between a tenuous Catholicism and middle-class culture on the one hand, and an increasingly influential culture of positivist thought and socialist ideas.

> It is therefore natural, and necessary, that in this terrible clash, those who lack the intellectual potential to adapt to new ideas, feel that their consciousness is so shaken that they are often literally dragged down to the point of voluntarily taking their own lives.[59]

Thus, the social dimension of suicide and its relationship to modern society and the state is broached. In fact, the psychology of suicide, timeless in its apparently personal and psychosexual dimensions, was only one area of concentration among the many turn-of-century investigators concerned with why so many Italians seemed to be trying to kill themselves. As Altavilla himself suggested, sociological and historical factors were also to be reckoned with in the national attempt to understand this "necessary" vice which had reached apparently epidemic proportions. Altavilla's use of the word "necessary" indicates that many Italians believed that epidemic suicide was also endemic. In other words, many Italians saw the apparent epidemic of suicide and some other forms of violence as being unfortunately integral to and not simply disruptive of certain historically specific aspects of Italian culture and society in the five decades from national unification in 1861 to World War I in 1915. The following four chapters will cover this broad range of social, cultural, historical, and political investigations and interpretations of suicide in this formative period, when what it meant to be an Italian was a topic of fierce national debate.

Notes

[1] Paolo Cesarini, *Tutti gli anni di Tozzi* (Montepulciano: editori del Grifo, 1982). p. 41.

[2] *Il Corriere della Sera*, Feb. 14, 1910, p. 6, "*Suicida in Carrobio.*"

[3] *La Nazione*, Sept. 29, 1913, p. 4, "*Tentato suicidio.*"

[4] *La Gazzetta Ferrarese*, March 24, 1911, p. 3, "*Ancora una giovanetta che tenta avvelenarsi.*"

[5] *Il Resto del Carlino*, Bologna, Nov. 22, 1906, cited in Enrico Altavilla, *La psicologia del suicidio: intuizioni psichologiche, documentazioni artistiche* (Naples: Perella editore, 1910) pp. 48–9.

[6] Altavilla, *La psicologia*, p. 49.

[7] Altavilla, *La psicologia*, p. 49, citing Louis Proal, *L'education et le suicide des enfants* (Paris: Alcan, 1907).

[8] Georg Simmel, "The Metropolis and Mental Life," in Donald Levine, ed., *On Individuality and Social Forms* (Chicago: University of Chicago Press, 1971), pp. 324–39; orig. pub. as "*Die Grosstadt und das Geistesleben,*" Berlin, 1903.

[9] Simmel, "Metropolis," p. 325.

[10] Simmel, "Metropolis," p. 336.

[11] Honoré de Balzac, "The Girl With the Golden Eyes," *History of the Thirteen*, trans. Herbert Hunt, (London: Penguin Books, 1978), p. 310; orig pub., *Histoire des Treize* (Paris, 1833–35).

[12] Altavilla, *La psicologia*, p. 69.

[13] Enrico Ferri, *Omicidio-suicidio: responsabilità giuridica* (Turin: Bocca, 1895), p. 129.

[14] Altavilla, *La psicologia*, p. 70, citing unspecified studies by unidentified authors Casper and Strassman.

[15] Altavilla, *La psicologia*, p. 70, citing an unidentified author Tamburrini, "*Ossessioni sessuali,*" *Rivista di freniatria e di medicina legale* (n.p., n.d.), vol. XXIII, p. 613.

[16] Emile Zola, *La Bête Humaine* (1890), English trans. and introduction by Leonard Tancock (London: Penguin Books, 1977), p. 9 for reference to Lombroso's influence; Cesare Lombroso, *L'uomo delinquente* (Milan: Hoepli, 1876), English version, *Crime: Its Causes and Remedies* (London: Heinemann, 1911); Gina Lombroso-Ferrero (Lombroso's daughter), *Cesare Lombroso: storia della vita e delle opere* (Bologna: Zanichelli, 1921); Luigi Bulferetti, *Cesare Lombroso* (Turin: Unione tipografico editrice torinese, 1975); Giorgio Colombo, *La scienza infelice: il museo di antropologia criminale di Cesare Lombroso* (Turin: Boringhieri, 1975), for a photographic display of Lombroso's body parts collection; Max Nordau, *Degeneration* (Berlin, 1892); Daniel Pick, *Faces of Degeneration: A European Disorder, c.1848–c.1918* (Cambridge: Cambridge University Press, 1989), esp. pp. 109–154 on Lombroso; and the more than 60 such forensic studies by Lombroso and his contemporaries in the *Biblioteca Antropologico-Giuridica* series by Bocca publishers, including, for example, M.L. Patrizi, *La Fisiologia d'un Bandito* (1904) and Ettore Fornasari di Verce, *Il Marinaio Epilettico e la Delinquenza Militare* (1896). Degeneration was a popular international literary theme, as evidenced in such diverse works as Nathaniel Hawthorne's *The Marble Faun* (1860), set in Rome; J.-K. Huysman's À *Rebours*, English trans., *Against Nature*

(1884); and all the works, for example, of Lombroso's contemporary Italian warrior-aesthete Gabriele d'Annunzio. See Barbara Spackman, *Decadent Geneaologies: The Rhetoric of Sickness from Baudelaire to d'Annunzio* (Ithaca: Cornell University Press, 1989). The Viennese architect Adolf Loos ("Ornament and Crime," 1908) based his disdain for stylistic ornamentation in degeneration theory. See also Robert Nye, *Crime, Politics, and Madness in Modern France: The Medical Concept of National Decline* (Princeton: Princeton University Press, 1984).

[17] Cesare Lombroso, *Genio e degenerazione* (Palermo: Remo Sandron, 1897); *L'Uomo di genio* (Turin: Bocca, 1894).

[18] Lombroso, *Genio e degenerazione*, p. 9.

[19] On Haeckel see Stephen Jay Gould, *Ontogeny and Phylogeny* (Cambridge: Belknap Press, 1977), p. 79 for Darwin's response. On the influence of Darwin and Haeckel in Italy, see Giuliano Pancaldi, *Darwin in Italy: Science Across Cultural Frontiers* (Bloomington: Indiana University Press, 1991; orig. *Darwin in Italia*, Bologna: il Mulino, 1983), esp. pp. 139–51 on Lombroso.

[20] Lombroso, *Crime*, pp. 442–443.

[21] Lombroso, *L'uomo di genio*, p. 66, citing figures attributed to an unspecified passage by Morselli.

[22] For example, C. Leggiardi-Laura, *Il delinquente nei 'Promessi Sposi'* (Turin: Bocca, 1899); G. Antonini and L. Cognetti de Martiis, *Vittorio Alfieri: studi psicopatologici*, with preface by Lombroso (Turin: Bocca, 1898); and M.L. Patrizi, *Saggio psico-antropologico su Giacomo Leopardi e la sua famiglia* (Turin: Bocca, 1896). The Baroque painter Caravaggio, the poet Tasso, the jurist Cesare Beccaria, Michelangelo, and the American author Edgar Allan Poe were the subjects of similar investigations.

[23] Altavilla, *La psicologia*, p. 67.

[24] Tertullian, "A Treatise on the Soul," cited in Thomas Laqueur, *Making Sex: Body and Gender from the Greeks to Freud* (Cambridge: Harvard University Press, 1990), p. 47, note 65.

[25] Altavilla, *La psicologia*, pp. 74–75, citing unspecified studies by an unidentifed author, Forel.

[26] Altavilla, *La psicologia*, p. 79.

[27] Altavilla, *La psicologia*, p. 79.

[28] Altavilla, *La psicologia*, p. 79.

[29] On changing terminologies and definitions of same-sex desire see David F. Greenberg, *The Construction of Homosexuality* (Chicago: University of Chicago Press, 1988), esp. pp. 397–433 for this period.

[30] Robert Aldrich, *The Seduction of the Mediterranean: Writing, Art, and Homosexual Fantasy* (London: Routledge, 1993); Michael Rocke, *Forbidden Friendships: Homosexuality and Male Culture in Renaissance Florence* (New York: Oxford University Press, 1996), for the Florenzer attribution; James M. Saslow, *Ganymede in the Renaissance: Homosexuality in Art and Society* (New Haven: Yale, 1986); and Herbert M. Schueller and Robert L. Peters, eds., *The Letters of John Addington Symonds: Volume I, 1844–1868* (Detroit: Wayne State University Press, 1967), esp. letters dated Oct. 10, 1890, p. 507; July 1891, p. 587; Sept. 30, 1891, p. 612; May 2, 1892, p. 685; June 20, 1892, p. 694; and Jan. 15, 1892, p. 650. In the last letter Symonds describes his poignant

visit in Aquila, in the remote Abruzzi region east of Rome, with the self-exiled German homosexual rights activist Karl Ulrichs.

[31] Giulio Crivellari, *Il codice penale per il regno d'Italia* (Turin: Unione Tipografico-editrice,1889), Article 331, p. 127.

[32] Crivellari, *Il codice* (1889), p. 123.

[33] For example, Florence's *La Nazione*, Oct. 3, 1913, *"L'arresto di uno straniero"* ("Arrest of a Foreigner"), for *"atti sconci,"* p. 3.

[34] Cesare Lombroso, *Crime: Its Causes and Remedies* (London: Heinemann, 1911), p. 418, revised trans. of *L'uomo delinquente*. See also case no. 10, *"Pederasta pazzo criminoso,"* examined by G. Virgilio, in S. Ottolenghi and V. Rossi, *Duecento criminali e prostitute: studiate nei laboratori di clinica psichiatrica e di antropologia di Torino*, with preface by Lombroso (Turin: Bocca, 1898); Ivan Bloch, *La vita sessuale dei nostri tempi nei suoi rapporti con la civiltà moderna*, Italian trans. of 10th German edition/4th Italian edition (Turin: Societa' tipografico-editrice nazionale, 1912), with an appendix of three chapters by Lombroso, titled *"L'amore nel suicidio, nel delitto e nella pazzia,"* orig. pub. as *L'amore nel suicidio e nel delitto* (Turin: Loescher, 1881); Arrigo Tamassia, *Sull'inversione dell'istinto sessuale* (Reggio Emilia, 1878).

[35] Lombroso, *Donna delinquente*, p. 254; and further examples pp. 254–70.

[36] Lombroso, *Donna delinquente*, p. 493.

[37] Lombroso, *Genio e degenerazione*, p. 67.

[38] Scipio Sighele, *La coppia criminale: studio di psicologia morbosa* (Turin: Bocca, 1892), p. 137.

[39] Sighele, *La coppia*, p. 138.

[40] Sighele, *La coppia*, p. 142.

[41] Enrico Ferri, *Omicidio-suicidio*, p. 9; pp. 256 and 272 for charts by Ferri's colleague Scipio Sighele and others.

[42] Richard Krafft-Ebbing, *Psychopathia Sexualis* (Stuttgart: Enke, 1889 edition; orig. pub. Berlin, 1882), pp. 216–19, as cited in Eric Rofes, *I Thought People Like That Killed Themselves* (San Francisco: Grey Fox Press, 1983), p. 5, and p. 140, note 17. For a currrent understanding of the documented links between suicide and repression of same-sex desire see Rofes's study as well as Gary Remafedi, James A. Farrow, and Robert W. Deisher, "Risk Factors for Attempted Suicide in Gay and Bisexual Youth," *Pediatrics*, vol. 87, no. 6, June 1991, pp. 869–875.

[43] Ferri, *Omicidio-suicidio*, p. XXIII.

[44] See Jeffrey Weeks, " 'Nature had nothing to do with it': the role of sexology," in *Sexuality and Its Discontents: Meanings, Myths, and Modern Sexualities* (London: Routledge & Kegan Paul, 1985), pp. 61–95.

[45] Altavilla, *La psicologia*, p. 201. For background see Arthur J. Droge and James D. Tabor, *A Noble Death: Suicide and Martyrdom Among Christians and Jews in Antiquity* (New York: HarperCollins, 1992); Clayton J. Drees, "Sainthood and Suicide: The Motives of the Martyrs of Cordoba, a.d. 850–859," *Journal of Medieval and Renaissance Studies*, 20:1, (Spring, 1990), pp. 59–89; Gary Dickson, *"The Flagellants of 1260 and the Crusades,"* Journal of Medieval History, 15 (1989), pp. 227–267; Norman Cohn, *The Pursuit of the Millenium: Revolutionary Millenarians and Mystical Anarchists of the Middle Ages*, (New York: Oxford University Press, 1961); A. Alvarez, *The Savage God:*

A Study of Suicide (New York: Random House, 1970), pp. 66–75; and the 12th-century lauds of Jacopone da Todi and Saint Francis of Assisi, as well as, for example, Taddeo Di Bartolo's San Gimignano frescoes of 1396.

[46] Altavilla, *La psicologia*, p. 67, citing Giovanni Enrico Meiboni (physician, 1590–1655), *"Epistola de flagrarum usu in re venerea et lomborum rerunque officio"* (n.d.).

[47] Altavilla, *La psicologia*, p. 71.

[48] Altavilla, *La psicologia*, p. 161.

[49] Altavilla, *La psicologia*, p. 167.

[50] Lombroso, *La donna delinquente*, p. 355.

[51] *La Gazzetta Ferrarese*, March 24, 1911, *"Tra il Vecchio e il Nuovo: Misericordia Immorale,"* p. 1.

[52] Cesare Lombroso, *La donna delinquente, la prostituta, e la donna normale* (Turin: Bocca, 1893; revised by his daughter Gina Lombroso-Ferrero, 1915); S. Ottolenghi and V. Rossi, *Duecento criminali e prostitute: studiate nei laboratori di clinica psichiatrica e di antropologia criminale di Torino*, with preface by Lombroso (Turin: Bocca, 1898); and among many female studies of the more than sixty contemporary *Biblioteca Antropologico-Giuridica* publications, for example, R. Guerrieri and Ettore Fornasari di Verce, *I Sensi e le Anomalie Somatiche nella Donna Normale e nella Prostituta* (1893).

[53] Giulio Crivellari, *Il codice penale per il Regno d'Italia* (Turin: Unione tipografico editrice, 1889), Articles 353–358, p. 132.

[54] Giulio Crivellari, *Il codice penale per il Regno d'Italia* (Turin: Unione tipografico-editrice, 1890; vol. 7, 1896, ed. Giovanni Sumann), Articles 331–339, pp. 472–563. Crivellari's brief, preliminary 1889 study was supplemented in 1890 with the first of a multi-volume set of studies of the Zanardelli reforms, the later volumes of which were edited by Giovanni Sumann.

[55] Lombroso, *Crime*, p. 417.

[56] Lombroso, *La donna delinquente* (1915), p. 485.

[57] Altavilla, *La psicologia*, p. 144.

[58] Altavilla, *La psicologia*, p. 144.

[59] Altavilla, *La psicologia*, p. 298.

2. A Civilizing Safety Valve

In 1878—twenty years before the publication in France of Emile Durkheim's classic study of suicide—the Lombard Royal Institute recognized the phenomenon of increasing personal self-destruction as a growing threat to the new Italian nation and sponsored a competition for the best new investigation of why so many Italians seemed to be killing themselves.[1] Enrico Morselli, then director of the insane asylum at Macerata in the central Adriatic region of the Marches, submitted the winning entry from among what had become a cottage industry of Italian suicidologists. Morselli's 500-page tome, *Suicide: Comparative Study of Moral Statistics*, was in fact just one of some 133 suicide investigations known to have been published in Italy between 1850 and 1889.[2]

The Italians, however, were not unique in their concern over suicide. Emilio Motta's *Bibliography of Suicide*, published at Bellinzona in the Italian-speaking Swiss canton of Ticino in 1890, lists 647 entries on suicide published mainly in Europe from the 16th through the 19th centuries.[3] With an offhand reference to the 1886 drowning suicide of Bavaria's mad Ludwig II, who as a known sexual "invert" was a favorite topic of degeneration theorists, Motta prefaces his extensive list by noting that it contains only major works, ignoring "that flood of boring verse which in recent years, along with romance biographies of German sovereigns who killed themselves, crowd the columns of the usual, low-brow Sunday papers."[4]

Some 419 of Motta's entries were published after 1850, with Italy's 133 books on the subject in that half-century indicating that the new nation was catching up with an earlier French and German domination of the field. Noting that "we live in the century of the bibliography," Motta acknowledged that the sheer volume of studies cited in his compilation indicated a modern obsession with statistics and classification as much as it demonstrated an interest in suicide itself.[5]

A survey of Motta's hundreds of entries supports Morselli's earlier observation of a historical trend away from traditional philosophical and religious condemnations and inquiries of suicide toward more ostensibly scientific investigations carried out by medical doctors and secular researchers.[6]

Motta further allowed that suicide had become an umbrella topic associated with any number of social anxieties and controversial issues.

Nationalism, sexuality, nostalgia, the military, hunting, biography, and the law are just a few of the sub-categories which dominate many of the 133 suicide studies Motta lists as having been published in Italy in the last half of the 19th century. Recognition of these subsidiary reasons for intense interest in suicide did not, however, dilute Motta's conviction that the problem was quantifiably real.

> Among the civilized nations of Europe suicide is so terrifyingly on the rise that it is catching up with birth and total death rates.[7]

Morselli and his contemporaries all worked from the same collection of official governmental statistics.[8] Before looking at aggregate numbers of suicides committed and increases in the suicide rate, however, it would be helpful to survey some general characteristics of the data itself. First, with regard to gender, suicide statistics from 1864 through 1905 show that about 80 percent of all Italian suicides were consistently committed by males. By the end of the period here under review, however, female suicide as a percentage of total Italian suicides had increased to roughly 25 percent on the eve of World War I.[9] Morselli suggested: "It is easy to understand the reasons for the great male preponderance of suicide."

> The difficulties of existence, at least those associated with vital competition, are more serious for men. Women participate in life according to their affections, and so even if they possess a more impressionable nervous system, they enjoy an ability to resign themselves to adversity with less difficulty. Self-denial is the pre-eminent feminine virtue, just as ambition is the primary masculine trait. And just as women are equipped with the necessary energy to confront the misadventures and delusions of life with that strength, men are especially at risk because they are less patient in the face of life's obstacles against the satisfaction of their desires.[10]

Serafino Bonomi, one of Morselli's many competitor-colleagues in the national contest to explain Italy's rising suicide rate, offered similar explanations of different suicide levels between men and women:

> As much as he is equipped with moral courage the male does not tolerate pain; and all too often, he abuses his free will, not simply to confront the problems of his life, but to rise to solutions, which the mild and tempered soul of the woman rejects.[11]

According to all of Morselli's various comparative indices, suicide rates were slightly higher for unmarried men than for married men, and relatively the same for married women and single females. Nevertheless, and without offering any definitive proof beyond the commonplace understanding that married couples enjoyed companionship, not to mention the legal and social benefits not available to the unmarried, Morselli and other investigators asserted "the statistics show how serious the damage is to the unmarried" who are deprived of "matrimony's beneficent effect."[12] Such analyses of suicide must be viewed within the context of prevailing contemporary condemnations of sexual relations not strictly defined by the norms of heterosexual marriage. Morselli and other suicide investigators simply accepted traditional social arrangements as innately rewarding, without entertaining the possibility that the proscription of alternatives could actively lead to more deaths by suicide among those individuals for whom marriage—heterosexual or not—was neither legally possible nor appealing.

With regard to age, males and females were both most likely to kill themselves while in their twenties.[13] These suicides in the third decade of life constituted the single largest suicide age group and consistently accounted for about a quarter of all Italians who took their own lives. This figure may have contributed to Morselli's comments on the benefits of marriage, given his notation that in Italy "only 11 of every thousand males gets married before the age of 20," while the comparable figure among women was 164 per thousand.[14]

In the period from 1866 to 1915 teenage girls accounted for an increasing percentage of total female suicides, rising from just over 7 percent in 1866 to more than 16 percent on the eve of World War I. Over the same half-century, teenage boys comprised a relatively stable 5 to 7 percent of all male suicides. Among males, percentage suicide rates by age group did not begin to significantly decrease until the age of 60. Female suicide percentages by age group, however, dropped significantly with the passage of each decade from the age of thirty, except among widows. Even as he acknowledged that widowers were more likely to commit suicide than widows, Morselli interpreted the figures to mean that "as widows, women are brought closer to the male social condition," especially when "the death of a husband leaves the widow with the added burden of providing for children."[15] As with the discussion of the benefits of marriage, these characterizations of the social position of the wife and the widow, however accurate they may be, beg the question of whether the stigma of being a single mother—even if nobly widowed—did not carry its own active inducement to suicide, as opposed to the notion that such a transition simply made a woman's obligations more like those of a man.

Statistics for the period under review also show suicide to be much more common in the North than in the South, and in urban rather than rural areas.[16] Culturally, the North-South difference fit into Morselli's observation that suicide was more frequent in Protestant or religiously mixed societies than among more strictly Catholic areas.[17]

Furthermore, the North-South difference would fit neatly into degeneration theory since researchers such as Lombroso held that the South, in all categories of human and economic development, had not evolved as fully as had the North. In an 1888 pamphlet titled *Troppo Presto* (*Too Soon*) Lombroso objected to proposals for what would become Italy's first uniform penal code, arguing: "Italy is united, but not unified." To clarify his point Lombroso asserted that a murder in the South was not the same thing as a murder in the North, claiming: "Italy is not joined as one, even in evil."[18]

Morselli also cites homicide statistics showing an average higher murder rate for the South, in support of the theory that homicide and suicide are related inversely. "Where crimes against property predominate," according to Lombroso, "suicide is more common than in those regions where blood crimes are more frequent."[19] Morselli also linked the higher homicide rate and lower suicide rate in the South to documented mass illiteracy, just as he argued that the North's opposite tendency in both categories is a result of "the parallelism, which exists between the expansion of culture and voluntary death."[20] By the time Morselli had compiled his suicide statistics it was still generally true, especially in the South that no more than three per cent of Italians spoke the officially sanctioned Italian language, with most daily conversations and transactions being conducted in any number of local dialects and unwritten tongues.[21] None of the explanatory models of suicide as a sign of "expansion of culture" makes any sense, unless degeneration theory and its malleable categories—which explain everything and nothing—are employed.

Beyond these cultural explanations offered for such regional disparity, the difference of numbers of suicides between North and South also begs the question of whether all of these numbers are not skewed by the fact that the northern, urban societies generally kept more meticulous social data (except for ecclesiastically documented sacraments such as parish records of baptism, first communion, confirmation, marriage, and funerals) especially on a taboo subject such as suicide, than did the rural, more thoroughly Catholic southern regions.

Among the myriad other categories of statistical documentation, Morselli included data on lunar phases and *"influenze cosmico-naturali,"* or "natural cosmic influences," which showed higher suicide rates, especially among women, during the full moon.[22] Morselli showed that in both the North and the South, suicides occurred more frequently in spring and early summer.[23] These observations were accompanied by the speculative pronouncement:

> It would be useful to investigate whether barometric variations, as well as humidity and wind measurements, along with other meteorological phenomenon such as rainstorms, tornadoes, hurricanes, and lightning and electrical storms, being chemical states of the atmosphere, do not coincide with the oscillation in the number of suicides, as Lombroso has proved in the case of the insane and epileptics.[24]

As noted in the previous discussion of degeneration theory, such sweeping generalizations and affirmations of standardized "insane" and "epileptic" human psycho-somatic types were taken to be an advanced, enlightened antidote to traditional superstitions and religious beliefs because they were thought to be scientifically based in quantifiably measurable data. Such analyses were thought to offer more compassionate understanding and potentially curative relief for those unfortunate "degenerates" who through no fault of their own had failed to share in the successful evolution of the human race at large. Ferri's emphasis on "the criminal (a real living person)" rather than "the crime (an abstraction)" merits being repeated here. This was not the first such clash in Italian history between competing reformist and traditionalist authorities, all of whom thought that their own methods of treating aberrant behavior and illness were the best way of doing good, as the history of conflict between Church and public health officials during outbreaks of bubonic plague had illustrated.[25]

Among his many other categories of investigation, Morselli also claimed his figures showed that women in general chose less demonstratively violent methods of self-destruction than did men.

> The major difference is in drowning and the use of firearms. It can be said that in Italy almost half of the women and a quarter of the men seek their deaths in

water; suicides by pistol or shotgun constitute a third of male suicides, but only a thirtieth of the females. The preference of the stronger sex for weapons includes sharp, cutting objects, also popular among women. Among women, in addition to drowning, there is a greater tendency than among men to commit suicide by jumping, poisoning, and suffocation; while men more often throw themselves to be crushed under trains. Hanging constitutes about the same proportion of total suicides in both sexes.[26]

With regard to place and method of suicide, Morselli's disciple Enrico Altavilla spoke some years later of a southern Italian town on a plain perched against a deep river, arguing that some locations were simply by definition suicidal:

The chance suggestiveness of a place does not just influence the means of death, but often initiates the very idea of suicide.[27]

As was already noted with regard to Lombroso's genius-related assertions on higher suicide rates among literary men and lower rates among the uneducated, the overwhelming number of Italian suicides were committed among the common working people for the simple reason that they comprised the overwhelming majority of the population. Among the conscripted and career military, however, which Morselli characterized as by definition "the most robust and healthy" sub-group of all Italians, suicide rates were alarmingly high.[28] Without citing precise sources, Morselli states that from 1871 through 1875, a five year total of 32 military officers were known to have killed themselves, out of an annual average 11,316 officers in uniform, resulting in a figure of 565 officer suicides per million. Among lower ranks, 230 suicides took place in the same period, for a corresponding figure of 276 per million. And among the mass of conscripted troops, 262 suicides were recorded, for an official figure of 294 per million. To dramatize his concern, Morselli further elucidates that these figures show that suicide among members of the military is "ten times that of the general civilian population, five times that of men in general, and four times that of males between the ages of 20 and 30."[29]

Arguing "this is not the place for detailed discussion" of military procedure, Morselli at least partially attributes the high suicide rates to "distance from one's hometown and disgust with military life, especially the rigid discipline." He notes that all of Europe's militaries had high suicide rates compared with civilian suicide. Durkheim and, more recently Minois, confirmed that Italy's military suicide rate was the highest in Europe during this period. Furthermore, in contradiction of assumptions that military suicide might be a response to rough conditions of military life, Morselli's own figures, cited also by Durkheim, showed that suicide rates were curiously more than twice as high among officers than among conscripts.[30] This surprising difference may represent the importance of honor and reputation among the officer corps and will be further addressed (Ch. 5) in the context of the duel as a form of indirect suicide.

Morselli also comments briefly on suicide in prisons, where the male suicide rate in 1872 was 160 per million inmates. The female rate, among an unspecified but significantly lower total number of inmates, was 680 suicides per million. Morselli cites the isolation and harsh conditions of prison life, as well as shame as leading causes of such suicides, especially among unmarried inmates. These explanatory models again beg the related question posed by Lombroso's formulation of the nature of "born" as opposed to "occasional" homosexuals with regard to the frequency of voluntary or forced same-sex relations in army barracks and institutions of same-sex confinement. Morselli's silence on this issue is as revealing as is Lombroso's attention to it.[31]

In addition to focusing on some of Morselli's statistical readings of the suicide phenomenon and his colleagues' insights on why so many Italians were killing themselves, it would be helpful now to look at the actual raw numbers and rates of suicide in Italy in comparison also with international statistics regarding this "necessary" epidemic. As Morselli noted, suicide statistics had been collected in the regions of Italy's expanding national territory only since 1864, three years after the still-fragmented nation had been officially united. Moreover, these early figures were "incomplete and lacking uniformity," especially given the fact that Rome, under centuries of papal control, was not annexed as capital of the nation until 1870. Even then, it would be many decades before uniform legal and civil practices were established throughout the whole country.[32]

Therefore, Morselli and other suicide investigators all worked from an unreliable but official base count of 836 suicides known to have occurred in Italy in 1871, the first full year following political unification. Over the succeeding four years, from 1872 through 1875, the official number of Italian suicides increased to 890, 975, 1,015, and then dropped slightly to 922. In 1876 the official suicide count jumped to 1,024, and then skyrocketed to 1,139 in 1877. This was the last year of available figures for studies, such as Morselli's, which were entered in the national competition.[33]

    With a total population of just over 28 million in 1877, Italy's suicide rate in this last year of Morselli's study was, by his account, 40.6 per million inhabitants. The comparable figure for 1871 had been 31 suicides per million inhabitants, rising steadily to 33 in 1872, 36 in 1873, and 37 in 1874. The figures dropped slightly, to 34 per million in 1875 before resuming the upward trend for a count of 36.5 per million in 1876. It was this proportional rise from 31 suicides per million inhabitants in 1871 to 40.6 per million in 1877, which alarmed Italians.[34]

    By way of international comparison, Morselli cited similarly "incomplete" suicide statistics for England, showing a rate of 66 suicides per million inhabitants in 1871, rising to 73 per million in 1876.[35] Enrico Ferri's more complete statistical charts on the subject, published in 1895, showed that with a total population of about 26 million in 1871 and 29 million in 1877, England registered 1,495 suicides in 1871, with a slight rise to 1,699 suicides in 1877.[36] Thus, suicide rates in the cradle of the industrial revolution were comparatively high by Italian standards, but relatively stable at 57 and 58 per million inhabitants over the period from 1871 to 1877. Morselli clearly linked rise in suicide rates to liberal economic and political development:

> Suicide became more common in England from the moment it stepped to the forefront of the development of European civilization, with the great acquisition of political and individual freedoms, and as the leader in world commerce.[37]

    According to this analysis, England's "immense wealth" was accompanied by a "terrifying misery, even worse than that found in less wealthy and adventurous nations." Anticipating Simmel's later description of the social effects of modern life, Morselli suggests the resulting "distinctions of social class were enough to provoke an increase in crime and suicide, either out of despair over unfulfilled desire and ambition, or because of the huge increase in psychic activity."[38] In order to explain the relative constancy of England's suicide rate at the time of his research, however, Morselli asked rhetorically,

> Could it be that the tendency toward suicide progresses to a certain level and then stabilizes itself?[39]

In France, which like England was an industrializing power and had been a sovereign nation for centuries, Morselli found further "uncontestable" confirmation of "the general laws of statistical progression of suicide."[40]   Praising France's extensive, centralized system of census-taking and data-gathering, Morselli noted a steadily increasing suicide rate, from 48 per million as far back as 1827, to an average of 150 per million in the period from 1871-1875. Enrico Ferri's more complete charts of 1895 show an even higher average, with the number of suicides jumping from 4,490 in 1871 to 5,922 in 1877. Given a total population of about 36 million in 1871 and 37 million in 1877, France's suicide rate according to these figures thus rose in just over five years from 124 to 160 per million inhabitants.

In a curious side comment, Morselli further noted that "exceptions to the law of regular progression" in French suicide figures for this period occurred in 1830 and 1847.   In 1829-1830, suicides dropped slightly from 58 to 54 per million, only to rise to 63 per million in the politically tumultuous year of 1831. Similarly, though in reverse direction, suicides in 1846–1847 jumped from 88.7 per million to 103.7 per million, then dropping to 93.5 per million in the yet again politically revolutionary year of 1848. By 1849 the comparable figure stabilized at about 100 suicides per million inhabitants, increasing regularly, however, from 1855 onward.[41] Without distinguishing between increases or declines in the numbers, Morselli asks:

> Could these oscillations be explained by the political agitations that occurred in 1831 and during the revolution of 1848?[42]

Morselli failed to ask the same question, however, of the even more politically volatile period on either side of the Franco-Prussian war and the Paris Commune during 1870–1871, when suicide statistics did in fact diverge temporarily from the regular pattern of steady increase. However scientifically unsatisfactory or theoretically incomplete Morselli's anecdotal observation may be, later statistical data for Italy at the beginning and end of World War I, early in the Fascist regime, and after World War II, all show similar oscillations which may or may not reflect politically associated social tension. Not surprisingly, official suicide figures dropped during the war years, only to proceed to regular patterns of increase at the cessation of conflict.[43]

Citing other contemporary European comparisons, Morselli noted that the newly unified but much more industrially developed Germany was experiencing its own modern surge in suicide, with figures in centrally important Prussia, which included the capital of Berlin, rising from 70 suicides per million residents in the distant period of 1816–20 to 133 suicides per million residents in the first five years of German unification from 1871 to 1875.[44]

Denmark, defined by Morselli as "the fatherland of Hamlet," was said to be "the classic land of suicide and the sad leader of all northern nations in this category," with a declining but stabilizing ratio of 258 suicides per million inhabitants in the period from 1871 to 1876. The period from 1861 to 1865 was Denmark's peak suicide time, at 288 such deaths per million, with just one million, six hundred thousand inhabitants. Morselli attributes the relative proportional decline after 1865 not so much to an actual drop in suicide cases as to an increasing Danish birth rate and the numerical effects of an infusion of a new refugee population following Germany's successful annexation of the contested Schleswig-Holstein province as a result of the Prusso-Danish war of 1864. Durkheim confirms Morselli's characterization of Denmark as the leader in suicide rates among European nations and notes further that the Danish military and civilian suicide rates were roughly equal.[45]

Noting the unreliable nature of the "very minimal statistical data we have for the Empire of the North," Morselli cites a variety of studies, which show a rise of suicide in Russia from 17 per million inhabitants in 1819 to 30 per million in 1875. These admittedly unreliable figures are introduced, nevertheless, with the curious explanatory note that suicide in Russia "is infrequent because of both the level of civilization and the nature of Russian society, as well as the hereditary apathy of the impoverished classes." Having made this confusing cultural generalization, Morselli immediately notes, however:

> Since the time of Catherine the Great, suicide had always served the serfs as a means of escaping the horrors of slavery.[46]

Among his many other comparisons, Morselli cast his statistical net across the Atlantic to the United States and Argentina. In each case he cited lack of reliable data due to "continuous immigration" which would obscure "the exact proportion between violent deaths and population" as reason not to take too seriously the reported figures. Sketchy numbers for New York City in 1845, for example, showed a decreasing ratio, down to 113 suicides per million inhabitants. The rest of the state showed a figure of 43 suicides per million, also a ratio in decline. In the period 1871–75, industrially developed Massachusetts officially registered 82 suicides per million inhabitants.[47]

Italian social observers such as the psychologist Altavilla, the criminologist Lombroso, the premier suicidologist Enrico Morselli, and the art and social critic Mario Morasso, among others, looked at these comparative international figures and linked the rise in reported suicides in Italy to the nascent processes of industrial modernization and late but culturally incomplete national unification, in which Italy was said to be anxiously following the lead of England, France, and Germany.

Italy's apparently galloping suicide rates paralleled the late but intense industrial 'take-off' hailed by the early twentieth-century philosopher-historian Benedetto Croce. Without addressing the suicide issue, Croce's *History of Italy, 1871–1915* celebrated "the accelerated rhythm that Italian life had taken," arguing that "no other European country in that period accomplished so much rapid and extensive progress as did Italy." With the same attention to statistical increase conveyed by Italian suicidologists, Croce proudly noted that the amount of coal imported for industrial expansion had doubled between 1900 and 1907; that 981 new steam-powered boilers had been manufactured in 1905 alone; and that "in 1900 in Italy six automobiles were made; in 1907, 1,283."[48] According to Croce's figures, Italian foreign trade increased by 118 percent between 1890 and 1907, compared with increases of 55 percent for England and 92 percent for Germany in the same period. Of importance here is the Italian perception that statistics showed their nation was catching up and closing in on its industrial precursors, experiencing what Alexander Gerschenkron later called the "advantages of economic backwardness."[49]

Writing ten years after Morselli's study and a good thirty years before Croce, the acclaimed Durkheim commented on the suicidal impact of such rapid economic development, when he noted:

So far is the increase in poverty from causing the increase in suicide that even fortunate crises, the effect of which is abruptly to enhance a country's prosperity, affect suicide like economic disasters.[50]

Citing Morselli's contemporary, Ettore Fornasari di Verce and his 1894 book, *Crime and the Economic Development of Italy*, Durkheim lists any number of economic indicators of perceived progress, including the assertion that between 1873 and 1889 salaries in Italy rose 35 per cent. Within this very period of apparently increasing financial prosperity, however, Durkheim—citing the same statistics used by Morselli and Fornasari di Verce—notes that from 1871 to 1877 suicide rates increased a roughly equivalent 36 per cent. And from 1877 to 1889 Durkheim notes an additional 28 per cent increase in suicide, in parallel increases in measurements of Italian economic development.[51]

Obviously, using 1871 as a statistical take-off date gives Italy a short-term boost when computing percentage changes of all categories of social data, given the longer statistically recorded histories of England, France and even Germany. As Motta noted, suicidologists like Morselli and his colleagues made endless and occasionally confusing use of comparative statistics as much out of a fascination with the possibilities of quantifying all aspects of an increasingly complex national life as out of any solid, scientific basis for the interpretation of these numbers. With these caveats in mind, it is nonetheless true that contemporary studies showed a precipitous rise in Italian suicide rates in the period from Unification to World War I.

Enrico Ferri's 1895 study, noting the author's debt to Morselli's earlier figures, goes on to provide a suicide census through 1890. The figures rise steadily each year from 1,261 in 1880, to 1,459 in 1885, to 1,653 in 1890. For the already-stated reasons, including shame, it is fair to assume these numbers are under-reported. Furthermore, without any explanation Ferri himself notes, for example, that his 1882 figures are missing all suicides committed in the entire, populous province of Rome. Despite such under-counting, later government statistics confirm the popular belief of the period that suicide was increasing in epidemic proportions, rising from 1,874 in 1895 to 2,040 in 1900 to 2,379 in 1905 to 2,880 in 1910 to 3,092 in 1915, the year Italy belatedly entered World War I.

Relying on official census data of total population numbering 32 million in 1901 and 34 million in 1911 we can calculate a rough suicide rate which continued to rise dramatically from about 63 per million inhabitants in 1901 to 81 per million in 1911. Broken down according to categories of sex, official figures show 51.6 male suicides for every million Italian males in 1871, rising to 127.8 male suicides per million males by 1915, when Italy entered World War I. Comparable figures for female suicides per million Italian females range from 11.6 per million in 1871, rising to 43.5 per million in 1915. The combined male-female number of suicides for 1915 was 3,092, for an aggregate of 85 suicides per million Italians.[52]

To illustrate the perceived nature of the crisis one need only note that while 2,754 Italians officially committed suicide in 1911, an only slightly higher number (3,431) of Italians lost their lives that same year in the hugely popular invasion of Libya.[53]

Adding to the sense of suicidal crisis was Italy's hemorrhaging rate of emigration during this very period, which was hailed by Croce, Fornasari di Verce, and others as a time of great national economic growth. In the first decade of national life, from 1861 to 1870, 27,000 Italians left the country; the following decade, from 1871 to 1880, official emigration numbers jumped six-fold, to 168,000. In the third decade of national life, from 1881 to 1890, 992,000 Italians moved abroad; the figure jumped again, from 1891 to 1900, to 1,580,000. And in the first decade of the new century, from 1901 to 1910, Italy approached its fiftieth birthday losing 3,615,000 of its citizens to foreign lands.[54] As the historian Dennis Mack Smith has portrayed this crisis:

> By 1876 a hundred thousand people were leaving Italy a year, by 1901 half a million, and in the single year of 1913, 872,000 people left the country, that is to say one person in every forty. By 1914 there were thus five to six million Italians living abroad as compared with thirty-five million inside Italy.[55]

From classical times through the publication of Thomas Hobbes' *Leviathan* in 1561 and beyond, states and social critics had either condemned emigration or looked upon such losses of its citizens as a kind of shameful, societal suicide. In this sense, the punishment of exile was a kind of enforced suicide. But given Italy's poverty amidst so much apparent economic growth, Enrico Ferri rose before Parliament in the spring of 1888, to address the spiraling emigration crisis with direct reference to the contemporary crisis of suicide. Ferri argued that Italy's legislators needed to address the plight of the nation's emigrants.

> Millions of honest poor people who, despite their moral and intellectual misery, which is no one's fault, but simply the historic moment we live in, have not become criminals, but have remained honest, and have no other recourse—not theft and not murder—except for emigration or suicide.[56]

In the context of the much vaunted national economic growth accompanied by such a poverty-driven exodus, secular critics such as Morselli, Lombroso, and the art and social critic Mario Morasso, among others, saw suicide as an inevitable price to be paid for Italy's late but rapid modernization. In keeping with the principles of degeneration theory, it was thought that each step forward along the path of economic development from a small-town, pastoral way of life to an urban, industrial existence created a nervous society populated by a significant minority of innately flawed individuals whose even more complicated social instability was triggered by so much sudden change. These were the "throwbacks," or developmentally arrested individuals whose incomplete recapitulation of their species' evolutionary progress made them incapable of adapting to the swift changes of modern life.

Morselli linked the rising rate at which Italians were taking their own lives to an unavoidable and ironic "uncivilizing" process of "becoming civilized." For Morselli, as would be argued more than two decades later by Simmel, this double-edged mechanism of *"incivilimento,"* which can be translated as both "civilizing" and "uncivililizing," was tied to the social and psychic dislocation and sense of confusion associated with those conditions which some call progress and others experience as an extreme form of social dysphoria.

> We are the first to acknowledge the immense advantages that civilization brings to man, whether as material well-being or as psychic development; but let us not forget that every aspect of humanity can be both good and bad, and that alongside those who gather the benefits of civilization there are also those who are pushed even further to degenerate physically and morally.[57]

Similarly, the critic Mario Morasso, in agreement with Altavilla's argument that suicide was a "necessary" corollary of modern development, asserted it was inevitable that the number of suicides would "increase with civilization and economic well-being."[58]

Enrico Ferri's charts indicate that even though Italy was experiencing a rise in its suicide rate, it stood statistically on a par with economically undeveloped Spain and Ireland as having more homicides than suicides. Meanwhile, France, Prussia, England, and Belgium had reached a point where suicides outnumbered homicides, reflecting their modern, industrial power.[59] In addition to the previous examples regarding homicide and literacy statistics, Morselli cites the work of his colleague "the esteemed Dr. Bonomi, director of the Como insane asylum," to defend the theory that homicide decreased and suicide increased with the progress of civilization. Bonomi claimed that even though suicide rates were not yet surpassing homicide rates in Italy, suicide was on the rise and that "the tendency toward suicide requires a certain development, a certain level of civilization which if it is allowed to modify and corrupt the more natural instincts, leads to a more gentle behavior."[60]

Morselli also explained the inverse homicide-suicide ratio according to such contradictory, all-inclusive, theory:

> The criminal, for whom there is no purpose but to satiate his overwhelming needs of passion, will murder and rob another man; but the individual whose upbringing instilled a sense of duty will, instead of availing himself of these homicidal practices, use his own hands to cut off the lifeline of his own existence.[61]

As we have already seen, Lombroso argued:

> Suicide is opposed to homicide; it is a real safety valve, so that where the one increases the other decreases.[62]

This apparently verifiable statistical trade-off persuaded Lombroso to declare:

> Suicide is of real advantage to the security of the state.[63]

As has been seen, Bonomi, Morselli, Ferri, Lombroso, and their entire generation of reformist colleagues all believed that sound degeneracy theory, physiognomical measurements, and reliable statistical data proved that suicide rates increased and homicide rates decreased as civilization subdued the murderous impulse common to those individuals who were an anti-evolutionary throwback to primitive societies. At the same time, a reservoir of endemic degenerative destruction, percolating beneath the surface of an increasingly restrained and civilized society, was thought to release itself in the act of suicide. But it was argued that suicide was not always committed in overtly recognizable suicidal ways. In addition to the kinds of obvious suicides, which were the primary focus of contemporary investigations, it was also thought that there existed a separate category of "indirect suicides." These suicides by apparently non-suicidal means might be thought of as the obverse of the girl who masturbatorily killed herself in the mirror really hoping to make it seem as if she were being murdered by a lover at her own consent. Enrico Ferri addressed the issue, suggesting:

> It is natural, indeed, that as the number of suicides increases and the number of homicides declines, with some exceptions, the numbers of indirect suicide, which is an intermediate metamorphosis between homicide and suicide, will increase.[64]

Ferri argued that certain violent activities were a masqueraded or "indirect suicide," and that many of these destructive behaviors which rid society of unhappy citizens were in fact "an intermediate stage of metamorphosis from homicide to suicide."[65]   According to Ferri's analysis:

> Indirect suicide can come about in two different ways: the first, which is most common in the psycho-pathological world, consists of a homicide committed with the exact intention of getting killed, especially as a result of the assumption that you will be condemned to capital punishment.

> The other, more frequently noted these days, and which has less to do with current psychiatric jargon, concerns the deliberate murder of an individual by someone who does not have either the physical or moral strength to simply kill oneself.[66]

The contemporary social commentator and literary critic Scipio Sighele supported Ferri's assertions on the relationship of "indirect suicide" and capital punishment, arguing even more forcefully that a contagious reaction of public violence and an adulatory cult of criminality might be the unintended results of the state putting people to death.

> It has been argued the danger of public executions consists in the fact that the spectacle of this horrible drama might reawaken the primitive yeast of savagery and cruelty, which gestates in a latent state in every individual.

> This is true, but there is another perhaps less serious but more immoral danger that the public might admire as a hero the murderer who knows how to stay serene in the face of the executioner.[67]

Enrico Altavilla was also in complete agreement with these expert opinions on the suicidal allure of capital punishment and the suicidal nature of some homicides in which the murderer kills a victim who is in fact a stand-in for the life of the killer himself. It could be argued in this sense that such a suicidal homicide which then led to the execution of the suicidal murderer would constitute a "double" suicide in which the perpetrator essentially managed to have killed himself twice. Speaking of this suicidal impulse to commit a crime as an act of self-destruction and of the added wish to then shift to the state the burden of doing away with one's own life, Altavilla argues:

This is exactly why in those countries that still have the death penalty so many criminals stump off their own dismal existence so frequently, and end up 'committing suicide' by committing crime.[68]

Altavilla then cites characters from Gabriele D'Annunzio's contemporary novel *The Triumph of Death* to illustrate the "psychological dualism" which incites such "indirect suicide," noting: "Giorgio Aurispa murders in order to kill himself, and Habibrach kills himself in order to murder."[69]

These arguments about "indirect suicide" and against capital punishment were especially useful in the contemporary debate over what could be done to stem a limited but resurgent popularity of the duel. Social reformers such as Piero Ellero, Francesco Crispolti, the jurist Giulio Crivellari, and Ferri himself, characterized dueling as indirectly suicidal behavior, echoing the French critic J.C. de Breyne's mid-nineteenth-century comment:

The duel consists, at the same time, of the perversity and the heinousness of both suicide and homicide.[70]

In *Omicidio-suicidio*, Ferri described the duel as a kind of suicidal search for honor in which "the generic and indirect consent of one's own death is carried out under the guise of an ostensibly well-mannered homicide."[71] In this context, Ferri briefly mentions contemporary Hungarian legislation, which placed the duel under suicide assistance statutes covering the killing of a consenting person.[72]

In contrast to the earlier example of the young girl whom Altavilla asserted had killed herself by slashing her throat in the mirror, in the desperate, masturbatory hope that she was being murdered by a lover-accomplice, Ferri's description of the duel and his own and Altavilla's depiction of certain criminal behavior as constituting "indirect suicide," leads naturally to the question of whether there were other ways of killing oneself without feeling to have done so or having it seem to be that one had not killed oneself since the death took place in an act of "honorable" violence. These and related issues will be further covered in the following chapters.

So far this study has surveyed the popular press for a feeling of public concern over suicide in the years spanning the turn of the century. Some contemporary psychological and evolutionary explanations for this perceived epidemic were then examined. Further statistical and sociological sources were reviewed giving credence to contemporary assumptions that suicide in Italy was indeed epidemic and catching up with the leveling rates of more industrially advanced societies. Contemporary observers were keenly interested in the erotic nature of suicide as well as in sociological explanations linking this 'endemic' epidemic of suicide to sudden economic growth and rapid urbanization.

We shall next review the position of the Church regarding the contemporary suicide epidemic, especially in the context of the historical divide and open hostility between the Vatican and the new Italian state. Then, some important historical and contemporary ecclesiastical, legal, and literary approaches to suicide in Italy will be examined. We will then conclude with a concentrated look at the duel, and how it was considered a form of "indirect suicide," with final thoughts on the place of war in the contemporary debate over suicide in this formative period of Italian national life.

Notes

[1] Emile Durkheim, *Le suicide: Etude de sociologie* (Paris, 1897), English trans., *Suicide: A Study in Sociology* (New York: Free Press, 1951).

[2] Enrico Morselli, *Il suicidio: saggio di statistica morale comparata* (Milan: Fratelli Dumolard, 1879). Other suicide investigations of the same general period included: Serafino Bonomi, *Del suicidio in Italia* (Milan: Vallardi, 1878); Mauro de Mauro, *Del suicidio e del concorso in esso riguardo al diritto di punire* (Catania: Bellini, 1876); Antonio Tagliabue, *Il suicidio* (Milan: Croci, 1871); Luigi Zuppetta, *Del suicidio in rapporto alla morale al diritto* (Naples: editore Anfossi, 1885); Concettino Sabatini, *Dello attentato all'propria vita* (Catanzaro: Calabro, 1902); Carlo Maria Curci, *Il suicidio studiato in se e nelle sue cagioni* (Florence, 1876), also reviewed in Curci's Jesuit review *Civiltà Cattolica*, Dec. 1876, series 9, vol. 12, pp. 714–16; Andrea Mondello-Nestler, *Il suicidio come delitto antinaturale ed anticristiano considerato nella sua origine e nei spaventevoli progressi* (Rome, 1877); Ferdinando Villani, *Il suicidio innanzi alla ragione e del diritto per l'avvocato* (Trani, 1866); Luigi Ricchini, *Tentati suicidi e suicidi con particolare riguardo alla città di Venezia* (Venice, 1903); Antonino de Luna, *Il suicidio nel diritto e nella vita sociale* (Rome, 1907); Geremia Bonomelli, *Il suicidio* (Rome, 1910); Gianmaria Fratini, *La patogenesi del suicidio* (Udine, 1910); Giuseppe Caponi, *Il suicidio: studio etico-giuridico* (Genoa, 1913); Vito Massarotti, *Il suicidio nella vita e nella società moderna* (Rome, 1913); Carlo Ravizza, *Il suicidio, il sacrificio della vita e il duello* (Milan: Branca, 1843); Matteo Liberatore, S.J., *Del diritto sulla vita per quel che concerne il suicidio, il duello, la pena di morte* (Naples, 1845); and previously cited Altavilla, *Il suicidio* (1910); Ferri, *Omicidio-suicidio* (1895); and on a lighter note, Paolo Ferrari, *Il suicidio: Commedia in 5 atti* (Milan, 1878).

[3] Emilio Motta, *Bibliografia del suicidio* (Bellinzona: Salvioni, 1890).

[4] Motta, *Bibliografia*, p.VI.

[5] Motta, *Bibliografia*, p V.

[6] Morselli, *Il suicidio*, p. 31.

[7] Motta, *Bibliografia*, p. V; Morselli, *Il suicidio*, p. 144, for statistical support.

[8] Some of the data used by Morselli and colleagues has been more recently reprinted in Stefano Somogyi, *Il suicidio in Italia, 1864-1965* (Rome: Tip. Olimpica, 1967).

[9] Morselli, *Il suicidio*, p. 294; Somogyi, *Il suicidio* 1967), pp. 18–19.

[10] Morselli, *Il suicidio*, pp. 298–99.

[11] Serafino Bonomi, *Del suicidio in Italia* (Milan: Vallardi, 1878), p. 26.

[12] Morselli, *Il suicidio*, p. 338; statistical tables pp. 340, 342–43.

[13] Morselli, *Il suicidio*, p. 311; Somogyi, *Il suicidio* (1967), p. 76.

[14] Morselli, *Il suicidio*, p. 334.

[15] Morselli, *Il suicidio*, pp. 342–43.

[16] Morselli, *Il suicidio*, pp. 98, 110–111, 273; Somogyi, *Il suicidio* (1967), pp. 28–29.

[17] Morselli, *Il suicidio*, p. 219.

[18] Lombroso, *Troppo Presto*, cited in Ugo Spirito, *Storia del Diritto Penale Italiano: Da Cesare Beccaria ai Nostri Giorni* (Rome: n.p., 1924; 2nd ed., 1932, repr. Florence: Sansoni, 1974), p. 141. See Gina Lombroso-Ferrero, *Cesare Lombroso: Storia della Vita*, pp. 264–67.

[19] Morselli, *Il suicidio*, p. 246.

[20] Morselli, *Il suicidio*, p. 227.

[21] Jonathan Steinberg, "The Historian and the *'Questione della Lingua'*," in Peter Burke and Ray Porter, eds., *The Social History of Language* (Cambridge: University of Cambridge Press, 1987), p. 198.

[22] Morselli, *Il suicidio*, p. 151.

[23] Morselli, *Il suicidio*, p. 103; p. 302; Somogyi, *Il suicidio* (1967), p. 57.

[24] Morselli, *Il suicidio*, p. 149.

[25] Ferri, *Omicidio-suicidio*, p. XXIII. For an earlier Italian conflict over diagnostic authority see, for example, Carlo M. Cipolla, *Faith, Reason, and the Plague in Seventeenth-Century Tuscany* (New York: Norton, 1981; orig. Bologna, Il Mulino, 1977).

[26] Morselli, *Il suicidio*, p 460.

[27] Altavilla, *La psicologia*, p. 98.

[28] Morselli, *Il suicidio*, p. 372.

[29] Morselli, *Il suicidio*, p. 376.

[30] Morselli, *Il suicidio*, p. 372; Durkheim, *Suicide*, p. 233; and Minois, *History of Suicide*, p. 300.

[31] Morselli, *Il suicidio*, p. 377–78.

[32] Morselli, *Il suicidio*, p. 84.

[33] Morselli, *Il suicidio*, pp. 54–55.

[34] Morselli, *Il suicidio*, p. 85.

[35] Morselli, *Il suicidio*, p. 67.

[36] Ferri, *Omicidio-suicidio*, p. 256.

[37] Morselli, *Il suicidio*, p. 64.

[38] Morselli, *Il suicidio*, pp. 64–65.

[39] Morselli, *Il suicidio*, p. 65.

[40] Morselli, *Il suicidio*, p. 78.

[41] Morselli, *Il suicidio*, p. 79; Ferri, *Omicidio-suicidio*, p. 256.

[42] Morselli, *Il suicidio*, p. 80.

[43] Somogyi, *Il suicidio* (1967), p. 19.

[44] Morselli, *Il suicidio*, p. 70.

[45] Morselli, *Il suicidio*, p. 61; and Durkheim, *Suicide*, p. 235.

[46] Morselli, *Il sucidio*, p. 62.

[47] Morselli, *Il suicidio*, pp. 91–93.

[48] Benedetto Croce, *Storia d'Italia dal 1871 al 1915* (Bari: Laterza, 1928), pp. 236–39.

[49] Alexander Gerschenkron, *Economic Backwardness in Historical Perspective* (Cambridge: Cambridge University Press, 1962), p. 86; and Valerio Castronuovo, "The Italian Take-Off: A Critical Re-Examination of the Problem," *Journal of Italian History*, vol. I, no. 3, winter 1978, pp. 492–510.

[50] Durkheim, *Suicide*, p. 243.

[51] Durkheim, *Suicide*, pp. 243–44, citing Ettore Fornasari di Verce, *La criminalità e le vicende economiche d'Italia* (Turin, 1894), pp. 77–83, 108–117, 86–104.

[52] For a full statistical breakdown, including the years following the work of contemporary suicidologists cited here, see Stefano Somogyi, *Il Suicidio* (1967), esp. pp. 18–19, 76–77.

[53] For Libyan casualties see Giorgio Candeloro, *Storia dell'Italia Moderna*, vol. VII (Milan: Feltrinelli, 1986), p. 329.

[54] B.R. Mitchell, *European Historical Statistics, 1750–1970* (New York: Columbia University Press, 1978), p. 47.

[55] Dennis Mack Smith, *Italy: A Modern History* (Ann Arbor: University of Michigan Press, 1959), p. 239.

[56] Enrico Ferri, *Appunti Parlamentari*, May 26, 1888, pp. 2982–2983, cited in Raffaele Colapietra, *Storia del Parlamento Italiano* (Palermo: Flaccovio editrice, 1976), vol. 9, appendix 3, p. 85.

[57] Morselli, *Il Suicidio*, p. 51.

[58] Mario Morasso, *L'Egoarchia: Uomini e idee del domani* (Turin: Bocca, 1898), p. 280.

[59] Ferri, *Omicidio-suicidio*, p. 272.

[60] Morselli, *Il suicidio*, p. 245, citing his colleague Serafino Bonomi, *Del suicidio in Italia* (Milan: Vaillardi, 1878), p. 21.

[61] Morselli, *Le leggi statistiche*, cited in Giacomo Canepa, "*La concezione Antropo-criminologica del suicidio,*" in Centro nazionale di prevenzione e difesa sociale, *Suicidio e tentato suicidio in Italia* (Milan: A. Giuffrè, 1967), p. 307.

[62] Lombroso, *Crime*, p.415; Canepa, "*La concezione,*" p. 307.

[63] Lombroso, *Crime*, p. 415.

[64] Enrico Ferri, *Omicidio-suicidio*, p. 9, citing numerous supportive studies by Sighele, and parliamentary commissions and charts; and Canepa, "*La Concezione,*" pp. 307–08.

[65] Ferri, *Omicidio-suicidio*, p. 9.

[66] Ferri, *Omicidio-suicidio*, p. 10.

[67] Scipio Sighele, *La coppia criminale: Studio di psicologia morbosa*, 2nd ed. (Turin: Bocca, 1897), p. 12; orig. pub. 1892.

[68] Altavilla, *La psicologia*, p. 57.

[69] Altavilla, *La psicologia*, p. 58; D'Annunzio, *Il Trionfo della Morte* (1894).

[70] J.C. De Breyne, *Du Suicide: considere aux point de vue philosophique, religieux, moral, et medical* (Paris: Rusand, 1847), p. 312.

[71] Ferri, *Omicidio-suicidio*, p. 106.

[72] Ferri, *Omicidio-suicidio*, p. 67.

3. A New Kind of Craziness Previously Unheard Of

Even as secular researchers like Altavilla called Jesus Christ a "suicidal" savior, contemporary Italian Church spokesmen condemned suicide as one of the many horrible practices, which they claimed had become fashionable and rampant as a result of the triumph of democratic ideas and practices associated with the French Revolution of 1789. The political unification of Italy as a secular state in 1861, and the annexation of Rome as Italy's capital, in 1870, were also seized on by Church defenders as a cause of the increased suicide rate.

In 1886, the Jesuit writer Luigi Previti, citing loss of faith and insatiable materialism as the roots of all that was wrong in modern life, specifically blamed the "revolution, which has become the matron of the *Bel Paese*" for the late 19th-century rise in Italian suicides.[1] Previti, and other Vatican advocates regularly published in the influential journal *Civiltà Cattolica*, pointed to the documented rise in the number of suicides in Italy since its unification as a modern state as proof that the "anti-Christian principles proclaimed in 1789" which "today are in command of Italy" were now taking a deadly toll on a citizenry victimized by "a new kind of craziness previously unheard of."[2]

Previti's analysis was based not only in a nostalgic defense of his Church's lost temporal power, but also in a genuine opposition to the new economic and social structure, which was developing in tandem with secular, political independence. Traditional, even feudal, relations were dissolving under the influences of modern life. From Previti's point of view, this revolution, which "makes laws and teaches that God need not be acknowledged," had inculcated atheism, materialism, and "a moral infirmity of the spirit" among the people. Previti argued that an "insatiable thirst for material gain, leisure, ostentation, pleasure, and lust" was integrally part of the new society in which individuals were led to "take pleasure in more than is economically or naturally possible."[3] Arguing that "not even the best individuals can stand up against" this new social order which has "made hardship intolerable," Previti asserts that all social classes are at risk for this inducement to suicide:

The poor no longer content themselves with their lot, and the rich vainly seek some satisfaction in this drunken stupor, which then degenerates into boredom.[4]

Previti concludes his attack on secular society and the new Italy saying that under such conditions as he has described, it is not surprising that so many individuals choose to kill themselves "cursing God as an illusion and the life hereafter as a fraud," while asking the futile question: "What's the point of doing anything down here?"[5]

However valid Previti's condemnation of gross materialism during this period may have been, it is important to remember that his analysis never specifically mentioned the new, galloping capitalism celebrated by Croce and others as the driving force of Italy's new economic power. But Previti did unequivocally and causally link destructively materialistic behavior directly with democracy and liberal principles of freedom associated with the French Revolution and the politically liberal—if incompletely realized—foundations of the new Italian state.   Other observers, such as the critic Morasso, were equally contemptuous of rampant materialism and vacuous ostentation, but saw such practices as a betrayal of the virtues of the French Revolution and the promises of the Risorgimento, or 're-awakening,' which had led to Italian Unification.

Morasso was especially critical of the burgeoning number of state-sponsored holidays and celebrations, which, he argued, led to a "collective drunkenness, fictive life, artificial excitement, and lack of memory."[6] The appeal of such celebration was, by Morasso's account, especially strong among the "plebian rabble, always the lover of uproar, parades, holidays, noise, and distraction regardless of their source or inspiration."[7] Arguing against this tendency for national identity to be defined through spectacle, Morasso said of his compatriots:

> Not content with the existing calendar of festivity, they seek new jubilees, centenaries, etc., creating new events inaugurating monuments, plaques, mausoleums, ossuaries; they unearth unknown celebrities, and forgotten memories, in order to form a committee, plan a program of celebrations, give an award, proclaim a series of speeches and win chilvalric honor.[8]

Morasso characterized the mood of Italians in this period as being one of passive citizenship influenced and maintained by what he describes as the mechanisms of a "bureaucracy of sentiment." Under this arrangement politicians and the people agreed on one principle:

> We do not want melancholy, sacrifice, and seriousness of work; these are not patriotic; we want to have fun and fool ourselves with speeches and holidays.[9]

In this context Morasso refers to the parliamentary debate in 1894 over whether or not to establish a national holiday on September 20, commemorating the taking of Rome from the Vatican on that date in 1870. Noting that at least one deputy argued against the proposal on the grounds that enough holidays already existed, Morasso flatly states that the purpose of the law was "either to affirm our right to Rome and revitalize the dormant civil enthusiasm of the Italian people, or to do nothing more than provide a new reason for a rise in the roving patriotic din."[10] Morasso further warned that the nation's *calendario festaiolo,* or "party calendar" was turning Italians into a "lazy people" not properly engaged in serious civic activity. Such observations reflected the Risorgimento patriot Massimo d'Azeglio's famous comment that given the enormous cultural, historical, and linguistic differences among the population, once Italy was united it would be necessary "to make Italians."[11]

Given his concern for the apparently degraded state of public life, it is interesting to observe that Morasso did not mention that as of 1861 the right to vote was restricted to a total of just under one-half million property-owning, primarily northern, literate males, constituting less than three per cent of the whole population. A later reform gave the vote to males over the age of 25 whose annual taxes were at least forty lire, whether they owned property or not. In 1882, voting lists were expanded to include a total of two million literate males over the age of 21, who, whatever their source of income, payed annual taxes of at least nineteen lire per year. Not until 1911 did property or income cease to be the sole basis for voting rights; but even then, suffrage was proclaimed "universal" only for males over the age of 30 or for male veterans of war of any age. Women would not gain the right to vote until the first free elections after the rout of Fascism many years later, in 1946.[12]

From its very beginning, the new Italian nation so vilified by Previti and others as being by its very existence the primary cause of the suicide epidemic, did not recognize a majority of its own citizens as being competent to participate in active political life. Morasso did not even imagine that this exclusion from the ballot box might help explain the popularity of patriotic demonstrations as the only way, other than in war, for non-voting citizens to participate in national life. Even Enrico Ferri, who lamented the dire economic conditions which forced so many Italians to choose between emigration and suicide, did not mention this lack of access to full civic participation as one potential contributing factor in the rising rate of both phenomena.

It must also be noted that then as now, most Italians were at least nominally Catholic, and that the overwhelming majority of Italians in this period were therefore constantly told by their Church that it was a sin to participate in the affairs of their nation. Conversely, the majority of Italian national leaders in the early years of the nation were by definition avowed deists, freemasons, agnostics, and atheists.[13]

Thus, average Italians swore allegiance to a nation, which did not permit them to vote and belonged to a church, which condemned the very existence of their country. According to some of the contemporary suicide analyses already discussed, these conditions might in themselves have contributed to a sense of popular detachment and alienation, leading to eccentric behaviors ranging from exuberant public celebration to epidemic private suicide. In 1881 the parliamentary deputy and future prime minister, Sidney Sonnino, touched on this mood of melancholy popular detachment, noting that a majority of Italians were essentially sad and "extraneous to our institutions."

> They see themselves as subject to the State and constricted to serve it with blood and money; but they do not feel that they constitute a living and organic part of it and they take no interest whatsoever in the state's existence and development.[14]

It is beyond the purview of this study of suicide in Italy during this period to fully investigate the history of Italian political unification and the Catholic Church's resistance to the Risorgimento and the new state. But a brief summary of some key facts in that history would fortify our understanding of the suicide debate, especially as we approach a discussion of suicide in contemporary literature, and Church and civil law.

The history of modern Italy being cobbled together piece by piece, with the capital established at Turin in 1861, moving to Florence in 1864, with Venice annexed not until 1866, and with Rome made capital in 1870, is a complicated story of romantic patriotism, domestic terrorism, and European war and diplomacy. By 1870 most of the modern Italian state, founded in 1861 under the diplomatic maneuvering of the very northern, French-speaking Count Camillo di Cavour and his sponsors in the French-speaking House of Savoy, had come to include Sicily, and most of the peninsula except for Rome, the nearby papal states, and the so-called "unredeemed" (terre irredente) lands in the extreme northeast.

These Germanic and Slavic *terre irredente*, situated on the southern side of the northeast geographic limit of Italian alpine territorial claims, were not clearly identified, linguistically or culturally, with the more patently obvious insistence that Rome be part of Italy.

By 1861, Naples and all the territories to its south had cast off their occupying Spanish dynasty; the Tuscan and other central Italian republics soon after voted to join the new union; Milan and its territory had been won from the Austrians even earlier in 1859; and Turin had already been the capital of the Savoys' Kingdom of Piedmont and Sardinia, which under Cavour's leadership had stitched the issue of Italian unification into every current war and peace treaty. As noted, Venice was not won from Austria until 1866, even as Nice, the birthplace of Garibaldi, and the French-speaking province of Savoy itself were ceded in territorial deals to France as early as 1860.

For the purposes of our study of suicide it is important simply to remember in this context that from 1861 until 1870 Rome and the nearby papal states had remained under temporal Vatican control, with the Church exercising secular power over the resident population. Thus, Rome and its scattered papal hinterlands, was literally surrounded by the rest of an independent Italy which had for most of a decade been freed from centuries of colonialist Austrian, French, and Spanish domination. Under these circumstances, the continuing papal governance of the most important city in the mythically eternal history of the peninsula was an affront to those who assumed that the destiny of Rome was that the old city would become the rejuvenated capital of a new, modern, secular nation.

But, as Previti's arguments made it clear, the final taking of Rome as Italy's capital was equally insulting to the Church, and gave cause for conjecture on all manner of the perceived degradations of contemporary mores and morality, with all social problems from then on identified with secular governance rooted in the principles of the French Revolution and Italian Unification.

Such fears of social decay linked to the rise of secular power were in keeping with the Church's existing political doctrine, outlined in the 1864 *Syllabus of Errors*. Promulgated by Pius IX, or Pio Nono as he was popularly known, the *Syllabus*, an addendum to the encyclical *Quanta Cura*, condemned freedom of discussion, religious toleration, and separation of church and state, as well as "progress, liberalism, and modern civilization."[15] This pontifical dictum only codified the Vatican's traditional opposition to secular Italian authority, which included de facto excommunication for anyone who dared participate in the politics of the new state.

Ecclesiastical opposition to the secular unification of Italy had evolved with special vehemence since at least 1848–49 when, in just the second year of Pio Nono's 32-year papacy, the people of Rome, like most of the rest of urban Europe, briefly rose up in a failed insurrection. The Holy City was declared a republic under the populist leadership of exiled Risorgimento militants such as Giuseppe Mazzini and Giuseppe Garilbaldi. Mazzini had been living in the sizeable London community of exiled unification advocates, while Garibaldi had been fighting as a soldier in South America on the side of independence movements against Spain. By July 1849 papal power over Rome was restored.

The possibly ironic explanation of Pio Nono's unconditional condemnation of the modern Italian state was that before the failed 1848–49 uprising, which had sent the young pope packing temporarily from the Vatican to Gaeta, midway to Naples, he had earned the skepticism of Europe's dynastic elites and won the tentative admiration of the "Young Italy" unification movement by giving amnesty to nationalistic political prisoners and granting a conservative constitution to his papal states. These youthful papal actions had even led to talk of Italy being ruled not by the existing, essentially foreign House of Savoy, but rather by a *papa re*, or pope king.[16]

By 1870 the Italian government based in Florence decided to take Rome by force. In 1860 the Piedmontese had blocked Garibaldi's planned invasion of Rome as premature. By 1870, however, the Vatican had little local support or international backing to rely on. Since the crushed revolution of 1848–49, the Vatican had depended not so much on its feeble Swiss Guards but on the presence of occupying French troops, or so-called *zouaves*, to protect its sovereignty. By the fall of 1870 French support of its Vatican mission was minimal and retreating. The defeat of France in the Franco-Prussian War of 1870–71, ending with the collapse of Paris under the triple weight of communard revolution, governmental assault, and German invasion ended foreign protection of the Vatican and emboldened the Italian monarchy and its parliament, meeting in Florence, to take the Eternal City.[17]

Rome thus "fell" at the centrally located Porta Pia on September 20, 1870, after a glorified street fight in which less than one hundred men died. One month later, in a plebiscite of 167,548 eligible male voters,

135,291 cast ballots on whether or not the liberated city should remain under Vatican control or go over to the Italian state. Of those 135,291 ballots cast, all but 1,507 voted to make Rome the secular capital of the new Italy, eliciting unsubstantiated accusations of voter fraud from Vatican apologists.[18]

This military victory did not resolve the cultural conflict between those who thought that the new state had done enough or had done too little with regard to the Church's absolute refusal to recognize Italy's existence. The contemporary poet Giosue Carducci described the lingering situation with reference to the *santa scala*, or holy staircase, adjacent to the Basilica of St. John Lateran, which served as the pope's personal church in his role as bishop of Rome:

> Oh, the entry into Rome; the government of Italy went up the triumphal path as though it were the *santa scala*, on its knees with a rope around its neck, crossing its arms and shouting 'Excuse me—I cannot help doing this—they have shoved me from behind.'[19]

As noted, the taking of Rome was not so much the last step of the unification process, but the first step in the challenge to give common governance and identity to a radically fragmented population spread across a highly diverse expanse of territory. Just as Lombroso had diagnosed the South and the North as existing at anthropologically criminal extremes of each other, any number of unification apologists bewailed the sorry state of Italian society as two nations divided. For example, in 1866, just as Venice and its territories had been won from Austria, the writer Pasquale Villari warned:

> Italy must now begin to recognize that she has at home an enemy, which is stronger than Austria. I refer to our colossal ignorance, our multitudes of illiterates, our machine bureaucrats, childish politicians, ignoramus professors, hopeless diplomats, incapable generals, unskilled workers, primitive farmers, and the rhetoric, which gnaws our very bones. It was not the Austrian garrisons in Mantua, Verona and the rest of the 'Quadrilateral' which barred our path, so much as our seventeen million illiterates, nearly a third of whom still live in truly arcadian simplicity.[20]

Enemies of Italian unification could take such honest self-appraisals as proof of the validity of Austrian statesman Clemens von Metternich's 1847 dismissive adage that "the word Italy is a geographical expression."[21] In fact, Metternich's quip was aimed at the then ostensibly 'liberal' Pio Nono's pre-revolutionary overtures to his temporal constituents, signaling the Austro-Hungarian Empire's official opposition to even the most conservative arrangements which might result in some form of Italian political independence.

In this context it is not surprising that Church fathers saw themselves as the one continuing authority capable of protecting Italian tradition and confronting the new, destabilizing conditions of commercial and civic life as society continued to evolve under the political rule of the modern nation. As early as 1876, two years before Morselli's winning entry was published in the civil competition to explain Italy's spiraling suicide rate, an in-house, favorable review of Monsignor C.M. Curci's book *Suicide: Its Bases and Causes*, appeared in *Civiltà Cattolica*. The review, which was unsigned and did not mention that Curci was the founder of *Civiltà Cattolica*, agreed with Curci's grim assessment of the growing popularity of suicide, asserting that the "ugly plague which in our era more than any other up to our own times, more than in any other previous period, contaminates our society."[22] It should be noted that Curci was later expelled from the increasingly virulent, anti-secular Jesuit order as he joined ranks with a growing minority of Church fathers who came to believe that the Vatican's interests were best protected by encouraging Catholic participation in the political institutions of the state rather than by simply condemning the modern world.[23]

Vatican and Jesuit hostility to Italian governance was especially vehement and regularly unleashed against Ernesto Nathan, the cosmopolitan, anti-clerical, London-born German-Italian Jew who served as mayor of Rome from 1906 to 1913. Nathan, who did not officially become an Italian citizen until the late age of 43, in 1888, was born in 1845 into a family active in London's Risorgimento circles. Nathan's father, Meyer Moses Nathan, was originally from the area near Frankfurt in what had not yet become Germany; his mother, Sarina Levi, was from the central Adriatic town of Pesaro in what had not yet become Italy. With twelve children, their London home was a lively place, made all the more so by the presence of Mazzini and other expatriated Risorgimento luminaries.

One year after Nathan's father died in 1859, his mother took the younger children, including the 15-year-old Ernesto, back to Italy, settling at Florence. After a period tutoring English in the Italian-Swiss city of Lugano, Nathan became active in the local Pesaro government of his mother's hometown. Once Rome had been taken, Nathan and his wife, Virginia Miele, moved to the new capital and made their home in the via Torino the city's most active, unabashedly secular intellectual salon, hosting Italy's most notable thinkers, writers, and liberal politicians. As a sign of his lifelong commitment to secular Italy on the part of this unlikely Roman mayor, it should be noted that Nathan volunteered and served in combat during World War I even though he was 70 years old, surviving to the age of 76 at his death in 1921.[24]

Drawing on classical understandings of Rome's historic destiny as a site of glory, decline, and resurgence, Nathan insisted that his secular capital was a "Third Rome of only one faith, that of the civil progress of Rome, capital of the Third Italy." Such declarations earned Nathan more than the usual Vatican assault on lay cultural and political figures; he was openly vilified in the pages of *Civiltà Cattolica* as "the Jew-Mason."[25] Nathan's Third Italy, and its Third Rome as secular capital city, was historically and physically based on the ruins of the First Rome of the Caesars and the Second Rome of the Popes. As Giuseppe Mazzini wrote in his 1845 tract *The Destiny of Italy:*

> The civil primacy twice exercised by Italy, through the arms of the Caesars and the voice of the Popes, is destined to be held a third time by the people of Italy—the nation.[26]

A decade before Rome finally came under secular rule, the southern parliamentary deputy and future prime minister, Francesco Crispi framed the "Roman question" within a discussion of the metaphorical health of the body politic:

> The question of Rome is vital. Rome belongs to Italy and must be our capital in order to calm the southern provinces. Rome is to Italy what the head is to the body; Rome must be taken because it has become a den of reaction, and so long as we do not have Rome, Italy cannot be tranquil.[27]

In this context, Nathan's unrepentant anti-clericalism and overt insistence on building a modern Rome consonant with the needs of a modern nation resulted in a persistent war of words over the role of the Church as both a religious force and a major property holder in the Eternal City. Nathan regularly referred to the Vatican as "an indigenous foreign power, which plots against us."[28] In response to Nathan's ambitious building plans for the city, including the completion of the so-called Altar to the Fatherland in the Piazza Venezia in central Rome, *Civiltà Cattolica* published regular broadsides against what was taken to be a wholesale physical assault on the theological, temporal, and urbanistic legacy of the architecturally elegant Second Rome of the popes.[29] The Vatican, steeped in Baroque splendor, knew very well the danger the secular state posed to its own traditions and self interests, not to mention its monuments. This is why Francesco Crispi made it clear to his parliamentary colleagues in 1881 that Rome was so important for both Italy's past and its future.

> We must build Italy in Rome if we want to stay in Rome, in a way that assures that the third life of this great city has to do with its past.[30]

For similarly secular, historical reasons Mario Morasso deplored the potential abuse of this nationalistic agenda when he critically observed:

> A showy tirade full of memories of Garibaldi, of martyrs, of epic poetry, of 'irredentism,' of 'Rome,' counts for more than a hundred laws, which would guarantee greater rights and an ingenious and rational educational order.[31]

It is in this historical context of Church antagonism to the victorious Risorgimental ideal of regaining the Eternal City as united Italy's secular capital that the suicide debate was played out. Central to this conflict was the Church's condemnation of the one overwhelmingly popular piece of literary fiction, which explicitly linked the struggle for Italian unification with suicide. While the Church centered its political attacks on the political tradition of which Ernesto Nathan was the most vocal, and local, advocate, Vatican apologists were just as quick to attack all expressions of contemporary, secular culture which were thought to threaten the well-being of the general populace. Ugo Foscolo's late-eighteenth-century epistolary novel *Le Ultime Lettere di Jacopo Ortis* (*The Last Letters of Jacopo Ortis*) wherein the narrator kills himself in a fit of reasoned passion, over unrequited love and unfullfilled possibilites of national unification, received special Vatican condemnation.

In a series of letters written over the year 1797–98 to his friend Lorenzo, the self-exiled, 24-year-old Jacopo Ortis agonizes over his own personal, romantic unhappiness and the frustrated political ambitions of his native northern Italy. It had been thought that the French Revolution of 1789 would spread a culture of enlightenment and democracy out from France across all of those European lands, which dreamed of republican, democratic governance. The revolution in Paris had instead produced a series of increasingly violent, reactionary regimes based more in suspicion and gamesmanship than in the heralded virtues of liberty, brotherhood, and equality.

Napoleon Bonaparte, a military officer with an uncanny ability to find career advancement amidst catastrophe, eventually came to power, and found himself finally exiled after 1815, far from Europe. But in 1797 Napoleon was a heroic military commander, carrying the initial call of the French Revolution's commitment to national independence and individual freedom across Europe. In northern Italy it was expected that Napoleon's invading forces would repel once and for all the occupying Austrians from Milan and Venice, and their surrounding territories. Instead, Napoleon signed the 1797 Treaty of Campoformio, allowing continued Austrian control of Jacopo Ortis's Veneto region in exchange for the liberation from Austrian control of Milan and its hinterlands.

Jacopo's hopes for a new fatherland were thus crushed by the very guarantor of the new European, nationalistic and allegedly democratic order. In the letters, which then constitute the entire epistolary novel, Jacopo Ortis reveals his personal and patriotic despair to his best and only friend, Lorenzo. Jacopo's heart is broken over an idealized, unrealizable love for a certain Teresa. And he has gone into exile, away from his native Veneto region, out of a simultaneous despair over his unrequited love and because of the squelched opportunity for the formation of an independent Italian nation. The theme of idealized, impossible love in Italian literature is as old as Dante's infatuation with the unattainable Beatrice and his theme of the *fino amore*, or "pure love," in his *Vita Nuova*. This literary trope and cultural ideal continued into the Romantic era in works such as Giacomo Leopardi's *A Silvia* and *Alla sua Donna*. In the case of *Jacopo Ortis* the theme of the impossible consummation of a love of a man for a woman is fused with Italy's evanescent quest for nationhood. Suicide is Jacopo's answer to this dual dilemma of unrealized heterosexual fulfillment and nationalistic identity, as when in his final note to Lorenzo, he addresses Teresa:

> And while you love me and I love you, and I feel that you will love me forever, do I leave you in the hope that our passion will burn out before the end of our days? No: just death, death.[32]

Jacopo's lamentations to his friend Lorenzo over his thwarted romantic and patriotic ambitions are couched in a description of his personal odyssey in search of "virtue," which had been fraught with a "fear of falling into vice." These comments are made within the context of repeated references to Lorenzo allegedly having written to Jacopo in terms indicating "you treat me as a beloved." An aura of repressed homoeroticism suffuses the correspondence in which romantic love is verbally communicated from one man to another, with the cover of a mythic female as the ostensible object of such affection.[33]

Jacopo Ortis's suicide note was written and sent to Lorenzo. But it was officially intended for Teresa. Jacopo's trail of sorrows, in which he sought virtue through the imposed solitude of his pure but impossible love for Teresa, was intended to protect him from being contaminated with "vice." At the novel's climax, Jacopo screams out against his lack of a woman and lack of a fatherland to whom he could give himself:

> If you had given me a fatherland, I would have spent all my genius and blood for you; and still, my weak voice has cried the truth courageously. All but corrupted by the world after having tried every one of its vices—No! These vices perhaps just briefly contaminated me, but they never conquered me—I sought virtue in solitude.[34]

In his *Civiltà Cattolica* article on suicide, the Jesuit Previti condemned Foscolo's novel and blamed it and other literary works, by Giacomo Leopardi and Antonio Guerazzi, for the contemporary suicide craze in Italy. Previti claimed:

> The history of suicide in Italy did not begin until that moment in which youth ran in crowds, infatuated with the writings of Ugo Foscolo, Giacomo Leopardi, and Guerazzi.[35]

Previti not only condemned the alleged popular effect of Foscolo's book on a susceptible Italian public. He went further, blaming the book and its author for the suicides of a whole generation. The novel had in fact been placed since its publication on the Vatican's *Index of Prohibited Books*. Previti accused Foscolo and his book of criminal incitement to suicide:

> How could we absolve the author of that infamous book of the crime of having shoved so many victims into the grave? No, truly, it is not possible to justify it! His death sentence is written in the blood of the history of those uncountable families drawn into the suicide of one of their loved ones.[36]

As a counterweight to any temptation to dismiss the outraged Previti simply as an aggrieved papist, no less an authority than Risorgimento hero Giuseppe Mazzini had recounted his own family's concern over his youthful, morbid response to Foscolo's literary creation.

> I childishly determined to dress always in black, fancying myself in mourning for my country. *Jacopo Ortis* happened to fall into my hands at this time, and the reading of it became a passion with me. I learned it by heart. Matters went so far that my poor mother became terrified lest I should commit suicide.[37]

This was the state and tone of discussion of such divisive matters in the period during which we have covered the problem of Italy's verifiably increasing suicide rate. Interestingly, little was said or written about what specifically could or should be done to stem the suicidal tide. More effort seems to have been given over to collecting data and wondering aloud how such horrific statistically verifiable facts could have come to inflict the *Bel Paese*. Suicide in this sense became a synechdoche, or vehicle for public debate, through which the much larger national discussions over what it meant to be an Italian, and what it meant to be a man or a woman, were carried out.

This public debate of suicide as a "site" of cultural contestation over definitions of personal and civic identity cannot be reified into an abstract linguistic or theoretical discourse over some hypothetical idea of what the debate over suicide "really meant." The discourse occurred and the cultural contestation happened because record numbers of individual human beings were choosing to kill themselves, possibly also for reasons of confusion over their own personal and civic identities. This brief study of suicide in Italy attempts to allow contemporary voices to speak on their own terms, while noting the silences, which might say as much about this crisis and the fears of addressing its root causes, as it reveals about what was actually said.

In the next chapter we will focus on the Church's theological tradition regarding suicide and the civil laws on suicide in the new Italian nation, with continuing reference to literary depictions of suicide and debates over capital punishment as an inducement to suicide. The final chapter will consider the duel as "indirect suicide" and the relationship of dueling, suicide, and war in light of the popular, contemporary notion that war was "the world's only hygiene."

Notes

[1] Luigi Previti, *"Il suicidio in Italia,"* *Civiltà Cattolica*, xiii, vol. 1, Feb. 1886 (Rome), pp. 513-24; this quote, p. 520.

[2] Previti, *"Il suicidio,"* pp. 523, 524, 515.

[3] Previti, *"Il suicidio,"* p. 524.

[4] Previti, *"Il suicidio,"* p. 524.

[5] Previti, *"Il suicidio,"* p. 524.

[6] Mario Morasso, *Uomini e idée del domani: L'egoarchia* (Turin: Bocca, 1898), p. 150.

[7] Morasso, *Uomini*, p. 154.

[8] Morasso, *Uomini*, p. 150.

[9] Morasso, *Uomini*, p. 151.

[10] Morasso, *Uomini*, p. 153.

[11] Cited in Denis Mack Smith, *Italy* (Ann Arbor: University of Michigan Press, 1969), p. 67; and A. William Salomone, *Italy from the Risorgimento to Fascism* (Garden City: Doubleday, 1970), p. 97. See also Giovanni Verga, *Novelle rusticane,* 1883.

[12] Denis Mack Smith, *Italy*, pp. 34, 107–08, 133–34.

[13] Denis Mack Smith, *Italy*, p. 222.

[14] Sidney Sonnino, in parliamentary remarks of March 30, 1881, cited in F. Chabod, *Storia della politica estera italiana dal 1870 al 1896* (Bari: Laterza, 1965), vol. II, p. 589; repr. in Emilio Gentile, *Il mito dello stato nuovo dall'antigiolittismo al fascismo* (Bari: Laterza, 1982), p. 3.

[15] Pius IX, *Syllabus of Errors* (1864), in Dennis Mack Smith, ed., *The Making of Italy: 1796–1870* (New York: Harper & Row, 1968), pp. 406–07; Denis Mack Smith, *Italy*, pp. 89–91.

[16] E.E.Y. Hales, *Pio Nono: A Study in European Politics and Religion in the Nineteenth Century* (Garden City, NY: Image Books/Doubleday, 1962); Denis Mack Smith, *The Making of Modern Italy, 1796-1870*, esp. pp. 110–45; and Priscilla Robertson, *The Revolutions of 1848: A Social History* (New York: Harper & Row, 1960; orig. pub. Princeton: Princeton University Press, 1952), pp. 309–401.

[17] See cabinet notes and narrative in Denis Mack Smith, *The Making of Italy*, pp. 408–12.

[18] Le Comte de Beauffort, *"Histoire de l'invasion des Etats Pontificaux et du Siège de Rome par l'armée Italienne en septembre 1870,"* Paris, 1874, pp. 392–400, in Denis Mack Smith, *The Making of Italy*, pp. 407–415, esp. p. 415 for plebiscite count.

[19] Giosuè Carducci, cited in Richard Drake, *Byzantium for Rome: The Politics of Nostalgia in Umbertian Italy, 1878–1900* (Chapel Hill: University of North Carolina Press, 1980), p. 11.

[20] Pasquale Villari, *"Di chi è la colpa?"* ("Whose Fault Is It?"), in *Il Politecnico* (Milan, September 1866), series IV, vol. II, pp 257–88, cited in Denis Mack Smith, *The Making Of Italy*, p. 395.

[21] Metternich, in Denis Mack Smith, *The Making of Italy*, p. 123.

[22] *Civiltà Cattolica*, *"Il suicidio,"* series 9, vol. 12, p. 714, reviewing C.M. Curci, *Il suicidio studiato in sè e nelle sue cagioni* (Florence: L. Manuelli, 1876), p. 714.

[23] Denis Mack Smith, *Italy*, p. 224; pp. 222–27 for a full depiction of the tentative, but incomplete accomodations made between the Vatican and Italy, especially under Pio Nono's successor Leo XIII.

[24] See Maria I. Macioti, *Ernesto Nathan: un sindaco che non ha fatto scuola* (Rome: Editrice Iuana, 1983); Richard Drake, *Byzantium for Rome*; Alessandro Levi, *Ricordi della vita e dei tempi di Ernesto Nathan* (Florence: LeMonnier, 1945); Istituto per la storia del Risorgimento italiano, *Roma nell'età giolittiana: L'amministrazione Nathan* (Rome: edizioni dell Ateneo, 1984).   On Rome in this period also see Alberto Carracciolo, *Roma capitale, dal risorgimento alla crisi dello stato liberale* (Rome: Rinascita, 1956); and Claudio Schwartzenberg, *"Fra storia urbana e storia giuridica: la capitale nell'età giolittiana,"* in Aldo A. Mola, ed., *Istituzioni e metodi politici dell'età giolittiana* (Turin: Centro Studi Piemontesi, 1979), pp. 251–62.

[25] Ernesto Nathan, *"La Terza Roma," Nuova Antologia*, Aug. 1, 1916; and *"Nathan: Ebreo-Massonico," Civiltà Cattolica*, vol. 2, 1911, p. 607–08; *"Il XX settembre: festa massonica," Civiltà Cattolica*, vol. 4, 1911, pp. 3–13, and item no. 4 of *"Cose Romane,"* p. 103.

[26] Giuseppe Mazzini, *"The Destiny of Italy,"* in Giuseppe Mazzini: *Selected Writings*, ed. N. Gangulee (London: Lindsay Drummond, 1945), p. 67.

[27] Francesco Crispi, in *Discorsi*, vol. II (1862), p. 691, cited in Caracciolo, *Roma capitale*, p. 191.

[28] Nathan, in Macioti, *Ernesto Nathan: un sindaco*, p. 32.

[29] See, for example, the unsigned *"Il XX settembre: festa massonica," Civiltà Cattolica*, vol. 4, 1911, pp. 3–13; Primo Acciarese, *Giuseppe Sacconi e l'opera sua massima: cronaca dei lavori del monumento nazionale a Vittorio Emanuele* (Rome: Tipografia dell'Unione editrice, 1911); Gianna Piantoni, *Roma 1911* (Rome: De Luca editore, 1980); and William Roscoe Thayer, "Italy in 1907," *Boston Evening Transcript*, April 27, 1907, repr. in Thayer, *Italica* (Boston, 1908; repr. Freeport, NY: Books For Libraries Press, 1969), pp. 307–46.

[30] Francesco Crispi, *"Discorso sulla legge per il concorso dello Stato nelle opere edilizie e di impliamento della capitale del Regno,"* Oct. 3, 1881, in *Discorsi*, vol. II (1862), p. 48, cited in Caracciolo, *Roma capitale*, p. 190.

[31] Morasso, *Uomini*, p. 150.

[32] Ugo Foscolo, *Le ultime lettere di Jacopo Ortis* (Milan: Mondadori, 1990; orig. pub. 1802), p. 133 (last letter to Teresa).

[33] Foscolo, *Ortis*, for example, pp. 23–26.

[34] Foscolo, *Ortis*, p. 133.

[35] Luigi Previti, *"Il Suicidio,"* p. 517.

[36] Luigi Previti, *"Il Suicidio,"* p. 517.

[37] Giuseppe Mazzini, *Life and Writings of Giuseppe Mazzini* (London, 1864) in Denis Mack Smith, ed., *The Making of Italy*, pp. 43–44.

4. We Do Not Call the Martyr Crazy

Religious critics like Previti and secular researchers like Morselli prefaced their remarks on contemporary suicide with brief references to the suicide theme in Italian history and literature. Special attention was given to the ancient Stoics' conditional acceptance of suicide, as depicted in the epic of the disgraced soldier Cato who chose to throw himself upon his own sword, and the dishonored wife Lucretia, whose wronged womanly honor was redeemed by her self-inflicted death.[1] Within the context of his criticism of the "heroic" suicide of Jacopo Ortis, Previti argued: "In no other time was taking one's life considered noble and virtuous." Previti further asserted:

> Even the Stoics in antiquity who were supportive of suicide did not pretend to give a sense of moral greatness to the act; they never made a hero of the individual suicide.[2]

Aside from these usual references to the Stoics, most critics, religious or secular, said little or nothing however, of the lamented but not always deplored depiction of suicide as the result of despair in the Renaissance and early modern works of later, revered writers such as Petrarch, Dante, Boccaccio, and the so-called *novellieri*. Dante reserved an especially awful fate for suicides in hell.[3]

As was indicated by the Church's response to *Jacopo Ortis*, religious and secular critics were especially concerned with the allure of suicide as portrayed in more recently published modern fiction. The decadent, suicidally-suffused works of Gabriele d'Annunzio were regularly attacked as "a nauseating invasion of sacred ideas" and "demented filth" in religious journals such as *Civiltà Cattolica*. D'Annunzio's *Martyrdom of Saint Sebastian*, written and originally performed in French during the author's expatriation in Paris from 1910 to 1915, was especially objectionable to the censors of *Civiltà Cattolica* because the centurion saint, iconographically pierced by arrows, was portrayed as a "pagan Adonis and androgynous *ballerino*."[4]

Secular critics such as Scipio Sighele and Enrico Ferri worried about the deleterious effects on the public of fictional, romantic suicides depicted in scores of popular novels such as D'Annunzio's *Triumph of Death,* George Sand's *Indiana*, Flaubert's *Madame Bovary*, Benjamin

Constant's *Adolphe*, and Goethe's *Sorrows of Young Werther*, the latter being considered the literary older twin of Foscolo's Ortis.[5]

Sighele and his colleague Enrico Ferri cite case after case of real and literary incidents in which a strong-willed "incubus" manipulatively seduces a weak "succubus" into committing "un-natural" and suicidal acts. Many of these cases involved botched double suicides in which either by accident or design the stronger "incubus" survives while the weaker "succubus" dies, unaware that his or her supposed pact has been betrayed. The survivor in cases involving a heterosexual couple was almost always the male.[6] Sighele feared that lengthy public trials and press coverage of such incidents would lead to actual copy-cat increases in the numbers of such suicides. The fear of literary suggestiveness as a source of epidemic suicide led Sighele to note:

> It has been said that there are pages of novels which can poison the organism like liquors, agitate the nerves like aphrodisiacal substances,and dull consciousness like narcotics. But it is also true that those who could read such pages without any threat, but indeed as a profitable experience, do not read them; and those who should be reading other things only read the pages they should never see. So, no lawsuits or indictments against the artist who from the heights of his genius has the sovereign and sacrosanct right to reproduce everything that exists in life; but we need an understanding and awareness to read and to recommend for reading only those certain books to those who can understand them, and only when such readings are well-advised.[7]

Within this same discussion of the power of art to influence life, Sighele quotes Victor Hugo as having admonished his fellow writers:

> Oh poets, always keep a moral vision. Do not forget children may read you. Have pity on the little blond heads. We must be more dedicated to youth than to age.[8]

On the contrary, in his preface to Enrico Altavilla's study of the psychology of suicide, Morselli argued against such theories of literary suggestiveness, asserting that such works of fiction simply reflected social reality:

> Under this approach it has been erroneously asserted that Werther and Jacopo Ortis gave birth to a trend, which raged through the young generation at the time they were published. By my account Goethe and Foscolo did nothing but to sense intuitively a deep and widespread state of social consciousness, and they impersonated this artistically in their literary characters.[9]

In this same preface to Altavilla's book on suicide, Morselli takes issue with the previously discussed great nineteenth-century melancholic poet, Giacomo Leopardi, who had argued:

> Now that heroism and illusions have disappeared and passions are weakened, the number of suicides is so much greater, not only among people known for their great sorrows and grand imaginations, but in every social group, such that these deaths are no longer renowned. This means that people are pondering, and wherever people ponder and meditate, without imagination or enthusiasm, life is detested; this is because an understanding of things as they are leads to a desire of death.[10]

To the contrary—Morselli wrote in response to Leopardi's "pessimism"—"men kill themselves for reasons of sentiment" which clouds their judgment of the true nature of things, rather than for lack of such imaginative sentiment that would mask the world's harsh realities. It could be argued that the hugely popular, contemporary Italian art form of opera dramatized this distinction most forcefully.

In fact, the dozens of operatic suicides—always female—most dramatically depicted in Giacomo Puccini's January 14, 1900 Rome production of *Tosca*, in which the doomed heroine throws herself from the battlements of Rome's Castel Sant'Angelo, escaped furious Church and secular criticisms. As Daniel Rolfs has suggested, Tosca and her suicidal operatic female cousins escaped the Church's wrath because they were portrayed as dissipated females battling overwhelming personal woes rather than as self-disciplined, heroic defenders of individual survival, even in death, of one person against society.[11]

In reality, Church and secular responses to suicide in real life and to its depiction in literature and the arts reflected longstanding cultural traditions and ecclesiastical and civic bodies of law which had evolved over centuries of debate over the ethics of taking one's own life.

As a matter of canon law, the Church, influenced by Augustine's condemnation of both the ancient Stoics and of suicidal Christian sects seeking salvation through martyrdom, had since the sixth century treated suicide as an eternally damning, mortal sin of "self-murder" resulting in deprivation of funeral rites and Christian burial. Against the alleged heroism of stoic Cato there was cast the long-suffering endurance of biblical Job; and against the image of Christ on the cross as a voluntary suicide, Christians were advised there would be no heavenly reward for a paraded martyrdom, which had been aggressively sought.[12]

In 1876 the Jesuit priest Curci, spoke of suicide as "the ugly plague, which more than in any other time contaminates our society." Addressing the indigenous Italian history of Stoic self-destruction, Christian martyrdom, and modern, Romantic suicide, which roughly paralleled the notion of a history of the "three Romes," an anonymous Jesuit reviewer of Curci's comments on suicide noted:

> Just as we don't call the martyr crazy, we don't call the taker of one's own life crazy, even if such acts deserve our condemnation; even if they were committed for reasons of honor.[13]

Ecclesiastical law, as developed since St. Thomas Aquinas's thirteenth-century *Summa Theologica*, went beyond the argument that suicide was a sin against God, the giver of all life, and incorporated Aristotle's position that suicide was also an act of hubris and betrayal of the *"polis,"* or community. Some Greek societies cut off the hand used by the person to kill himself, viewing the individual as a perpetrator of evil and instigator of emigrating tendencies against the community, rather than as a victim of tragic despair or self doubt.[14]

In medieval and early modern Christian Europe, corpses of suicides were routinely defiled, dragged through streets, and abandoned in garbage dumps or left with stakes in their hearts at crossroads beyond town walls, as both punishment for the betrayal of community and as a precaution against the suicidal individual's evil spirit returning to haunt the righteous living. Under such laws in vigor across most of Europe well into the nineteenth century, attempted suicide was a capital offense, punishable by death.

Though there is no evidence that such death penalties against people who had tried to kill themselves were carried out with any regularity in more recent modern times, as late as 1860 in London a man who had slashed his throat in an attempted suicide was hanged as punishment for his affront to society. When on the gallows the stitches to his wound opened, allowing passage of air in a kind of unintended tracheotomy, the unfortunate prisoner was lowered from his rope, stitched more tightly at the neck to guarantee asphyxiation, and hanged again—all for the crime of having tried to kill himself in the first place.[15]

Some of Italy's numerous pre-Unification regional statutes, which in the absence of a unitary national penal code were still on the books a quarter century after Unification, reflected a similar legal history of treating suicide and attempted suicide as a crime against society. Most notably, the politically important Sardinian-Piedmontese statutes, known as the *Codice Sardo*, contained provisions for punishment of suicide and attempted suicide. According to Enrico Ferri's summation, Article 585 of the 1839 *Codice Sardo* "punished the successful suicide by declaring the individual to be a coward, annulling any last will and testament, and depriving him of funeral rites; and whoever attempted suicide was condemned to jail for a term of from one to three years."[16]

On the opposite end of the legal spectrum, the equally influential *Codice Toscano*, in force in Tuscany in various forms since 1786, provided no punishment for attempted suicide, and neither banned funeral rites nor confiscated the inheritance of a suicide.[17] The Sardinian and Tuscan codes were similarly divergent in their approach to the question of what Sighele and Ferri had referred to as *omicidio-suicidio*, or homicide-suicide, wherein, as noted, an individual either directly participated in the alleged suicide of another person or acted to cause that person to take his or her own life. The revised *Codice Sardo* of 1859 maintained an "absolute silence on both homicide-suicide possibilities," while Article 314 of the *Codice Toscano* "punished 'participation in another's suicide with a jail term of from three to seven years."[18]

Ferri notes, however, that his own review of the legal literature in Germany, France, and Italy showed that other than a few convictions in such cases in Germany and even fewer in France, such homicide-suicide laws rarely resulted in actual jail terms, especially in Italy. Ferri suggests that in terms of "practical jurisprudence" most of such "double" homicide-suicide cases were never brought to trial. In those cases, which came to trial, verdicts were almost always either "absolved because of lack of evidence," or granted acquittal.[19] Citing the official *Italian Penal Judiciary Statistics for Tuscany* from 1880 to 1889, Ferri found only two prosecutions for participation in another person's suicide. Both trials ended without guilty verdicts, illustrating the difficulty of proving that a surviving individual in an alleged suicide tryst did not really intend to kill himself.[20]

Ferri's own legal opinion on the tangled issue of "homicide-suicide," and what in variations on the situation has since also been called "assisted suicide" was clear:

> I do not see such an enormous difference, as argued by classical criminologists, between the person who pushes someone to suicide and someone who kills a willingly suicidal individual. But, depending on the situation, it does seem that the person who gets someone else thinking about willfully killing himself ought

to be more subject to punishment than the person who simply carries out someone else's already determined decision.[21]

Ferri's legal position on suicide in this instance stems from his assertion that there is an underlying, fundamental distinction between public social interest and personal legal rights.

> It is an undeniable fact that society and the family have a natural interest in the existence of each of their members. But 'interest' is not the same as 'right' because the one traces its origins to simple 'usefulness,' while the other is based in the indiscernable concept of 'necessity.' Lacking this latter condition, there lacks the concept of a 'right.'[22]

For Ferri, this legal distinction between the tragedy of an individual's loss to his or her family by self-inflicted death and the society's interest in curtailing such flights from its ranks did not necessarily create a conflict between Church and state, however much his opinion on these matters may have differed in the details with official ecclesiastical points of view. Ferri elucidated his clear commitment to the risorgimental ideal of the complete separation of Church and State when he asserted:

> I would not even know how to give the state the right to defend my honor, my health, or my life even if I wanted to. Only the Church, which in logical coherence with its own principles, can pretend to save the sinner from his own depravity.[23]

Ferri made note of the fact that "of fifty penal codes I could examine only three even mention suicide"[24]. Russia, England, and the state of New York were so listed. In New York in this period, attempted suicide or assisted suicide carried a potential punishment of two years in prison or a thousand dollar fine, with such individuals trying to kill themselves defined as "guilty delinquents."[25]

In his evaluation of suicide and its legal implications Ferri mentions that during the period of his investigation hara-kari, or a falsified version of it was still common as a response to perceived lost honor in Japan:

> One killed oneself or had a friend kill yourself if struck by serious misfortune or if you had committed a dishonorable act.[26]

In this discussion of suicide Ferri made the curious but revelatory disclaimer and avowed claim of silence, tied to earlier analyses of violent behavior disguised as "indirect suicide," that he "will not speak of the duel."

> Because in the duel it is really true that there is a consent to one's own execution. It is a generic and indirect death, which has more to do with the method of one's own murder or injury than with the murder or injury itself.[27]

From the 1860s through the 1880s a succession of parliaments and committees wrestled with the legal status of suicide and "homicide-suicide," as part of the larger, project of creating a uniform national body of laws. In its first fully unitary penal code, adopted in 1889 under the leadership of justice minister Giuseppe Zanardelli, unified Italy rejected the *Codice Sardo* and adopted Tuscan precedents, decriminalizing suicide and attempted suicide. Under Title IX, Article 370 of the new legal code, suicide as the solitary act of an individual was not even mentioned; but prison terms of three to nine years were mandated for anyone proven to have caused or actively assisted in another's suicide. In its entirety the statute specifically states:

> Whoever causes or assists in another's suicide, when the suicide indeed occurs, is punished with imprisonment of from three to nine years.[28]

In parliamentary debate on the issue, Zanardelli argued against criminalization of suicide in legalistic terms based in the provisions of the esteemed Tuscan code. He did not, however, endorse suicide as an individual humanistic option as had Renaissance and Enlightenment writers such as Erasmus, Thomas More, Montaigne, John Donne, Voltaire, and David Hume.[29] Zanardelli declared simply:

> The history of criminal law shows that among the aberrations and absurdities of various legislation, there was even the criminalization of suicide, successful or not. If this is contrary to every healthy judicial principle, it is also true that the reasons, which justify not punishing the suicide do not apply to those who for maliciousness, financial gain, or misplaced mercy cause someone else to commit suicide or consciously assist in doing so.[30]

Making an even stronger distinction between legality and social acceptability of suicide some twenty years later, Enrico Altavilla argued:

> Suicide should be legally illicit and not tolerated, but not punished.[31]

CALIFORNIA INSTITUTE OF THE ARTS

In parliamentary debate over the new statute the decision to use the Italian verb *determinare*, or "to cause," rather than *indurre*, or "to induce," reflected unease over the difficulty in all but the most obvious cases of proving one person's definitive causative role in another person's suicide. Some anti-suicide advocates argued against Zanardelli's majority position, insisting unsuccessfully that suicide assistance be classified as one category of "voluntary homicide." Furthermore, the statute emphatically required that death actually occur, since—it was argued— attempted suicide in and of itself was no longer a crime.

This curious arrangement over what the Italians referred to as *mancato*, or "failed" suicide also reflected the earlier Piedmontese-Sardinian code which, as Zanardelli alluded, made no provision for punishment of suicide inducement or assistance even in the case of actual death.[32]

As has been earlier noted, the decriminalization of suicide under the Zanardelli reforms was accompanied by the abolition of capital punishment, the decriminalization of same-sex relations and of all consensual sexual relations between persons over the age of twelve, and a host of liberal penal reforms on issues ranging from slander, abortion, infanticide, adultery, homicide, the duel, and emigration. A shift away from absolutist prohibitions and universally rigid judicial norms to more moderate and flexible legal standards reflected three powerful forces which ran throughout the penal code debate and which are necessary pre-conditions for an understanding of the contemporary approach to suicide.

First, founding statesmen who had so recently lived under the autocratic rule of Italy's previous occupying authorities were in theory, if not always in practice, suspicious of overarching state power. Zanardelli himself argued that the state had an interest in enforcing law, order, and traditional family values even as he affirmed a lack of interest in deputizing the state as an enforcer of non-criminal social norms:

> If it is necessary on the one hand to severely repress activity which causes obvious and appreciable damage to the family or which is contrary to public decency, it is on the other hand also necessary that the lawmaker not invade the arena of morality.[33]

Second, by 1889 Italy was a nation extending from the Alps to Sicily, influenced especially by Tuscan republican traditions at odds with the more absolutist legal customs of both the Church and the founding

Kingdom of Piedmont-Sardinia. As the new nation gained the territories it had sought it was required to adopt and adapt to certain progressive regional laws and legal traditions, which, in the opinion of many legislators, could not be reversed. This was especially true in the debate over the abolition of capital punishment, which had resulted in twelve stalemated unitary penal code commissions, led by fourteen frustrated justice ministers by the time Zanardelli took on the project of overhauling the Italian legal system in 1887.[34]

Aside from the classical argument, popularized by Cesare Beccaria in 1764, that the state did not give life and so could not take it away, legislators argued in 1889 that it would be impossible to re-impose the death penalty in Tuscany, where it had been outlawed on and off again, with rare if any verifiable application since the enlightened reign of Leopold I in 1786, and definitively abolished by popular plebiscite since 1859.[35] The contemporary observer Giulio Crivellari interpreted the problem in these words, with regard to the challenge Tuscany, in its abolition of capital punishment, presented to the new nation:

> To complete unification it was necessary either to reintroduce the carnage in that province, or suppress the gallows elsewhere in the kingdom. The men of state were immobilized against this momentous situation. Free and independent Italy could not have reintroduced the sinister executioner where he had been chased away.[36]

The third, related reason for this shift from legal absolutism to flexibility in the penal code with regard to suicide and other aberrant behavior was the rising authority of scientific researchers such as Ferri and Altavilla, as well as their mentor Lombroso. Even if they were working from what would now be clearly recognized as a repressive pseudo-science, Lombroso and his disciples advocated rehabilitation and flexible penalties rather than uniform punishment of criminals. It must be remembered, however, that according to Lombroso's previously established definitions, men and women who by their behavior or scientific identification were regarded as "innately," or "born" homosexual or criminal were to be locked into the revolving door of the criminal jailhouse and the psychiatric asylum.

The rise to social and political prominence of these "positivist" reformers, such as Lombroso, Ferri, and Zanardelli, who advocated relatively mild punishment and individually tailored correctional sentences—compared with traditionally violent penalties for crime—

was especially remarkable given the fact that, as Crivellari noted, this was "a time in which a considerable part of the State was laid waste to and bloodied by a most brutally cruel political brigandage."[37]

It bears repeating in this social context of violence against the civilly constituted government that Scipio Sighele, whose research into suicide had led him to believe that certain acts of violence were in fact "indirect suicide," argued against capital punishment in Italy in this period, not out of concern for the soul of the duly condemned, but out of concern that capital punishment was a kind of state-sponsored suicide which would encourage further homicide.

> It has been said that the danger of public executions consists in the fact that the spectacle of this horrible drama might reawaken the primitive yeast of savagery and cruelty which gestates in a latent state in, every individual; this is true, but there is another perhaps less serious but more immoral danger that the public may admire as a hero the murderer who knows how to stay serene in the face of the hangman.[38]

In the next and final chapter we shall briefly investigate how the duel and certain types of agitation for and glorification of war might fit into this analysis of "indirect suicide," whereby suicidal men idealize fitfully held notions of personal worth and nationalistic pride in ways which lead them to seek their own deaths in the "honorable" activities of the duel and in war.

Notes

[1] Previti, "Il suicidio," pp. 516, 519; Morselli, Il suicidio, pp. 30–31; A. Alvarez, The Savage God: A Study of Suicide (New York: Random House, 1970), pp. 53–66, for a summation of the classical tradition.

[2] Previti, Il suicidio, p. 516.

[3] For suicide in Italian literature from antiquity through the 20th-century see Daniel Rolfs, The Last Cross: A History of the Suicide Theme in Italian Literature (Ravenna: Longo editore, 1981), esp. pp. 13–74 for antiquity through the 18th century; Alvarez, Savage God, pp. 143–148 on Dante; and Minois, History of Suicide, p. 33 on Dante, as well as generally on suicide in the Middle Ages and Renaissance.

[4] See the unsigned "Il Martirio di S. Sebastiano: mistero o mistificazione?" Civiltà Cattolica, vol. 2 (1911), pp. 651–669, esp. pp. 660–661 for this quote.

[5] See, for example, Scipio Sighele, Letteratura tragica (Milan: Treves, 1906), p. 212, and La coppia criminale: studio di psicologia morbosa (Turin: Bocca, 1892); Enrico Ferri, I Delinquenti nell'arte ((Genoa: Libreria moderna, 1901); Rolfs, Last Cross, pp. 75–108 on this Romantic tradition.

[6] Sighele, *Letteratura tragica*, p. 17; Ferri, *Omicidio-suicidio*, p. 281, and p. 93–139 for scores of such "double" cases, though mostly from outside Italy.

[7] Sighele, *Letteratura tragica*, p. 241.

[8] Victor Hugo, in Sighele, *Letteratura tragica*, p. 241.

[9] Morselli, in Altavilla, *La psicologia*, p. xviii; and Altavilla's assessment, p. 311.

[10] Giacomo Leopardi, *Scritti varii inediti* (Florence, 1906), cited in Morselli, pref. to Altavilla, *Psicologia*, p. xiv.

[11] Rolfs, *Last Cross*, pp. 109–110.

[12] Arthur J. Droge and James D. Tabor, *A Noble Death: Suicide and Martyrdom Among Christians and Jews in Antiquity* (San Francisco: HarperCollins, 1992), pp. 175–78 on Stoics, and p.1 and p.5 on martyrdom; Minois, *History of Suicide,* pp. 82–3; and Alvarez, *Last Cross*, pp. 66–73, for an overview of the Catholic position.

[13] *Civiltà Cattolica*, unsigned editorial, *"Il suicidio studiato in sè"* vol. 9. no 12, Dec. 1876, p. 715.

[14] Vincenzo Vitale, *"L'antigiuridicità 'strutturale' del suicidio,"* in Francesco D'Agostino, ed., *Diritto e corporeità: prospettive filosofiche e profili giuridici della disponibilità del corpo umano* (Milan: Jaca Book, 1984), pp. 121–45, esp. p. 126, n. 27 on Aristotle (*Nicomachean Ethics*), and n. 30 on Aquinas.

[15] Alvarez, *Savage God*, pp. 45–50; Droge and Tabor, *Noble Death*, p. 6; Rolfs, *Last Cross*, p. 64–65, n. 7; R.S. Guernsey, *Suicide: history of the penal laws* (New York: L.K. Strouse & Co., 1883); Forbes Winslow, *The anatomy of suicide* (London: H. Renshaw, 1840); and Minois, *History of Suicide*, p. 7, for torture of suicide corpse.

[16] Ferri, *Omicidio-suicidio*, p. 70.

[17] Ferri, *Omicidio-suicidio*, p. 69.

[18] Ferri, *Omicidio-suicidio*, p. 70.

[19] Ferri, *Omicidio-suicidio*, p. 92.

[20] Ferri, *Omicidio-suicidio*, p. 106.

[21] Ferri, *Omicidio-suicidio*, p. 66.

[22] Ferri, *Omicidio-suicidio*, p. 28.

[23] Ferri, *Omicidio-suicidio*, p. 54.

[24] Ferri, *Omicidio-suicidio*, p. 57, citing unspecified English law, and articles 1472–1476 of the 1866 Russian code, and articles 172–178 of the 1881 New York State code.

[25] Feri, *Omicidio-suicidio*, p. 178.

[26] Ferri, *Omicidio-suicidio*, p. 67.

[27] Ferri, *Omicidio-suicidio*, p. 106.

[28] See Giulio Crivellari, ed., *Il codice penale per il Regno d'Italia* (Turin, 1889) for a verbatim reprint of the new penal code, with limited commentary. For suicide provisions see Article 370, p. 141. For a fully annotated discussion of the new code and its history see Giulio Crivellari (vols. 1–5) and Giovanni Suman (vols. 6–8), eds., *Il codice penale per il Regno d'Italia*, 8 vols., (Turin: Unione tipografico editrice, 1890), esp. vol. I, pp. III–XXXVII on pre-Unification regional penal codes, and pp. CCXVII–CCCXIX on parliamentary debate of the new law.

[29] On the Renaissance and Enlightenment positions see Rolfs, *Last Cross*, p. 88, n. 18; Alvarez, *Savage God*, pp. 153–200; Erasmus, *In Praise of Folly* (1509); More, *Utopia*

(1516); Montaigne, *Essays* (1595); Donne, *Biathanatos* (1644); Voltaire, *"Du Suicide"* (1764); Hume, "Essay on Suicide" (1777).

[30] Zanardelli, *Relazione sul progetto di codice penale* (Turin: Unione tipografia editore, 1888, pp. 351–52), cited in Crivellari, *Il codice* (1890), vol. I, p. CCXCIII.

[31] Altavilla, p. 206, cited in Vitale and D'Agostino, *Diritto e corporeità*, p. 132.

[32] Crivellari, *Il codice* (1890), vol. VII (ed. G. Suman, 1896), pp. 831–832; and Vincenzo Patalano, *I delitti contro la vita* (Padua: CEDAM, 1984), pp. 206–07, n. 6–7, and pp. 226–227.

[33] Crivellari, *Il codice* (1889), p. 123.

[34] Crivellari, *Il codice* (1890), p. CLI.

[35] Cesare Beccaria, *Dei Delitti e delle pene* (Milan, 1764); Ugo Spirito, *Storia del diritto penale italiano: Da Cesare Beccaria ai nostri giorni* (Rome, 1924; repr. Florence: Sansoni, 1974), esp. pp. 41–58 on Beccaria, pp. 135–44 on Lombroso, and 155–70 on Enrico Ferri; Carlo Ghisalberti, *La codificazione del diritto in Italia, 1865–1942* (Rome: Laterza, 1985), esp. pp. 167–175 on Zanardelli; Elio Monachesi, "Cesare Beccaria," in Hermann Mannheim, ed., *Pioneers in Criminology* (Chicago: Quadrangle Books, 1960), pp. 36–50, orig. in *The Journal of Criminal Law, Criminology, and Police Science*, vol. 46, no. 4 (Nov.-Dec., 1955); Dino Carpanetto, "Tuscany in the Age of Leopold," in Carpanetto and Giuseppe Ricuperati, *Italy in the Age of Reason, 1685–1789*, trans. Caroline Higgitt, (London: Longman, 1987), pp. 210–222.

[36] Crivellari, *Il codice* (1890), p. XLII.

[37] Crivellari, *Il codice* (1890), p. XLII; pp. 46–59.

[38] Sighele, *Coppia criminale*, p. 12.

As has been documented in chapter two, Enrico Ferri, Scipio Sighele, Enrico Altavilla, and the French sociologist J.C. de Breyne, all argued that the duel was a form of "indirect suicide."[1] This take on the duel as a way of killing oneself without having to assume personal responsibility for one's own self-inflicted death was supported by the prominent French sociologist, Gabriel Tarde. The influential Tarde praised Ferri's book on suicide even as he complained: "the duel would have very well merited its honored place in this study, rather than such a brief allusion."[2]

Based on his understanding of the duel as indirect suicide, Tarde was reluctant to consider dueling as a crime, within the statutory framework of penalties for murder. For Tarde, the duel was at worst the "killing of a consenting individual," or "philanthropic homicide." Tarde was especially critical of the "monstrous" fact that in France, "every now and then the office of the public prosecutor, in the absence of special laws on this matter, charges honest duelists with homicide or attempted homicide."[3] Lombroso shared his French colleague's opposition to the criminalizing of the duel, arguing, "the duelist, at least in most cases, is rather a victim than a criminal."[4] Within this same context, Ferri looked to related non-Western suicidal practices:

> As is known, in Japan it was and still is common, if less frequently now, the custom of hara-kiri, in which it is considered a duty to kill oneself or have a friend kill you if you have been stricken with great misfortune, or have committed a dishonorable act.[5]

In Italy, hara-kiri, as such, was not practiced. But the duel, as an outlet for the vindication of lost honor or as a means of "indirect suicide," or both, was engaged in by a small but significant number of men during this period. Not surprisingly, a vast literature by both religious and secular critics emerged as the duel, in tandem with suicide and the debate over capital punishment, came to occupy public attention. Scores of secular critics wrote books and published hundreds of articles on dueling in the journal *Nuova antologia di lettere, scienze ed arti*, while the Jesuits at *Civiltà Cattolica* were also vigilant in their campaign against the duel, as they were in their crusade against suicide.[6]

78

As early as 1867, Antonio Tagliabue asserted: "The practice of the duel is spreading in the extreme across this land which was the mother of culture and civilization."[7]

Noting that he had written his study of the duel as a submission for an "open competition" on the subject sponsored by the Physio-Medical Statistics Academy of Milan, Tagliabue implored his compatriots not to "stand idly against this humiliating spectacle of so many duels which dishonor our beloved country."[8]   From his own religious perspective Tagliabue agreed with the "illustrious De Breyne" that suicide and dueling were related, arguing: "the principal and true causes of the duel are the same as those of suicide."[9]   As had been argued by clerics who confronted the issue of suicide, Tagliabue asserted that the apparent, contemporary surge in the number of duels being fought was the result of "a lack of religious faith" and "immersion in materialism and rationalism," which left people "disfigured in the slime of transitory pleasures, no longer believing in the future."[10]

Similarly, in a series of unsigned articles appearing in *Civiltà Cattolica* from 1896 through 1898, the "long and ever-increasing number of duels fought in Italy in recent years" was denounced.[11]   In June of 1896 the Jesuit journal cited official governmental statistics on "causes of death," indicating that from the second half of 1879 through the first half of 1895, 3,513 duels were known to have been fought in Italy. These duels resulted in 74 known deaths and 4,562 serious injuries. This report carried the warning that these figures were not exact, given that—as with suicide—many duels were never officially reported.[12]

Two years later, in the spring of 1898, *Civiltà Cattolica* updated its duel count, citing official, governmental statistics, which showed a new total of 3,679 duels known to have been fought since 1879. Of the 7,358 men who fought these duels, 78 died and 4,792 were seriously injured.[13]

Jacopo Gelli's 1928 study of the duel in Italy generally confirmed *Civiltà Cattolica's* figures. Noting the same problem of statistical undercounting common to suicide and dueling, Gelli identified average annual numbers of confirmed duels per year from 1879 to 1925. From 1879 through 1889, an average of 276 duels took place each year. From 1890 through 1900, the figure for duels was 116 per year. From 1901 through 1910, the average number of known duels per year dropped to 65. The duel figures dropped again to an average of 45 per year in the period from 1911 to 1915, when Italy belatedly entered World War I.

So, as the number of outright suicides rose in this period, the duel was in a state of resurgence followed by a phase of quick decline. During the war years, from 1915 through 1918, the statistical average number of known duels fought plummeted to two and one-half per year, meaning that only 15 duels were reported in the entire span of the war. This drop in dueling during war may not seem surprising, given the fact that in war, Italians were busier fighting their enemies rather than each other. The contemporary literature also suggests that those duels fought during war may also have been waged between military men whose honor in the wartime experience had been questioned. Earlier figures (Ch. 2) that enlisted men committed suicide less frequently than commissioned officers may also support the idea that dueling, like suicide, could only increase in frequency with a heightening of the perceived level of honor to be defended.

Beyond these speculative considerations, the concluding section of this chapter will consider how it may have been that the massive psychological and material mobilization necessary for a nation to engage in war provided a playing field of sacrifice in which suicide was indirectly committed under the honorable act of a patriotic death. The numbers, at least, support such a theory. In fact, once the war had ended, the duel resurfaced in Italian society, with an average of 74 face-offs occurring each year from 1919 through 1925, well into the Fascist era.[14]

As was the case with suicide, duel investigators plumbed their statistical sources, noting not only death and injury figures, but also seasonal tendencies and weapon preferences. Gelli made the curious observation that "the majority of duels in Italy take place in the summer, during the hot months, while in France the opposite is true."[15] This alleged seasonal aspect of dueling, it will be remembered, was also statistically shown to be true for Italian suicide, which peaked in summer months.

Just as suicide researchers also ranked the methods of death, from drowning to poisoning to hanging, for example, duel investigators such as Gelli and his colleague Angelo Coelli documented changing patterns in the weapons of choice among duelists. Sabers, followed by swords and then pistols, were the favored arms among Italian duelists in these years. Writing after World War I, however, Gelli noted that deaths in duels had decreased as a result of a gradual increase in the use of the less deadly and more easily handled sword, as opposed to the saber.[16]

To the question of "who engages in dueling?" Gelli's 1928 book answered: "a few of everyone," with a trend over the years of his survey showing an increasing number of journalists defending themselves against charges of slander by engaging in the duel.[17]   In his previous book on the duel, written four decades earlier in 1886, Gelli made special note of how "in these recent months, the plague of the duel has worsened not just a little in our army."[18] In his 1867 study of the duel, Tagliabue had wondered:

> Why are the leaders of our military so indifferent to the excessive habit of the duel among the officers? Why don't they raise their voice in reprobation and why don't they enforce statutes of the military code? Everyone knows that as things stand now the official who refuses to accept a duel challenge or assist in one otherwise is considered a coward, abandoned to the disdain of his colleagues.[19]

In his 1904 study of the duel, Angelo Coelli listed "nobles and military officers," as well as "all types of citizens of the upper-middle classes, especially professionals, such as lawyers, physicians, engineers, writers, scholars, judges, and journalists in particular," as constituting the types of contemporary gentlemen who engaged in the duel.[20]   This classification of who might engage in the duel is not surprising, given the fact that for honor to be defended it had to be first of all socially recognized or presumably possessed, as was by definition not possible for the lower classes who did not claim the prerequisites and perquisites of such recognized or presumed honorable gentlemen. As Coelli noted, journalists especially fell into such an ambiguous category, as they claimed a professional status for reporting the facts of democratic society at odds with an elite view of their work as scandal mongering, gossip-driven insubordination.

In his 1928 study of dueling, Gelli noted that the duel as a ritual restricted to the nobility had as a matter of social evolution been appropriated by those new socio-economic classes, which as a result of the French Revolution had ostensibly replaced the old aristocratic regime.[21]   In terms similar to Mario Morasso's critique of the popular mania for celebratory festivals, Gelli mockingly asserted:

> The bourgeoisie, having weakened the nobility, wanted to substitute personal character for force, and the power of ideas for the ways of the sword. But this was not a triumph of rights for that part of humanity which dominates the birth rate and the census, because the society which emerged from the Revolution

appropriated the old fetters of the defeated aristocracy; and while today they mock these noble titles, they also covet them and get all excited over any little trinket of a medal, even if bestowed on them by His Royal Majesty King Aurelio I of Patagonia and Aurocania.[22]

The Jesuits of *Civiltà Cattolica* made similar observations regarding the duel as an appropriation of discredited aristocratic ritual by ostensibly republican citizens. "Legislators, judges, and soldiers" who fought duels were compared to "princes of a royal house" because of their shared assumptions regarding their honor and the means by which they were entitled to defend it.[23] Among the worst offenders were members of the Italian parliament. In an 1896 article condemning the duel and its popularity among government officials, *Civiltà Cattolica* listed a dozen names of parliamentary deputies who were known to have engaged in duels either in combat or as witnesses "in the most recent months alone."[24] The most infamous of such parliamentary duels took place in Rome on March 6, 1898 when the parliamentary deputy Ferruccio Macola mortally wounded his legislator colleague Felice Cavallotti.[25]

As an impending discussion of the legal status of the duel in this period will help explain, the peculiar penal definitions of dueling, and the "Honorable" Cavallotti's parliamentary immunity allowed him to escape any questioning or punishment. Enrico Ferri was just one of scores of other members of parliament who were challenged to duel by their colleagues, though in one such instance he declined the affront, offering instead to let his challenger "feel the point of my boots."[26]

Just as the duel was, therefore, by definition a class-based institution for the adjudication of insult and the restitution of honor among nobles and the upper classes, it was also gender specific. Only males possessed such honor as might properly be defended in the duel. Women were by definition excluded from the entire moral, social, and legal definitions underpinning the institution of the duel. As Gelli noted:

> The female is recognized by all legal codes as being unfit for the duel, *impropre au duel,* and so, whatever offense may be directed against her does not so much strike her as it does injure, however, her natural protector.[27]

Gelli lists a hierarchy of male relatives, extending from husbands to fathers to brothers and to other male kin, whose honor is besmirched by attacks on their immediate women folk and female realtives, and who are, therefore, subject to the rules of the duel as a means of settling disputes over family honor. Similarly, Gelli notes:

The same obligations await the above-mentioned persons whenever their women provoke an offense rather than being the object of the offense.[28]

Within this developing context of the new nation sorting out its aristocratic past and attaching its republican aspirations and pretensions onto the persistent practices of the old regime, Gelli asserted:

The duel is based on the social prejudice that honor is not washed except in blood; but this prejudice falls short of determining exactly the amount of blood necessary for such purification.[29]

The expansion of dueling from the privileged ritual of an elite aristocracy into the common enough rite of a well-off fold of the populace had also led to a wave of dueling not unto death but to swords dropped at the first sign of injury. These duels were referred to as *duelli a primo sangue*, or "duels of first blood." While such duels fought between Italian men of rank did not fit into the contemporary German and Austrian fads of college boys sparring with swords in search of a romantically treasured facial scar, they did indicate an anxious embrace of heroic gesture coupled with an avoidance of the fatal price such gestures might incur.[30] As early as 1886 Gelli argued that dueling had become yet another way for increasingly anonymous citizens of the new industrial, urban society to differentiate themselves from their neighbors.

Duels of 'first blood' have become a vain, boyishly childish way to bicker over complaints. One goes onto the fighting field, not to guarantee one's honor so besmirched by the insults of one's adversary, but rather to make oneself at least notorious, if not interesting, when in other cases this would not be possible.[31]

Such duels, intended to bring attention to oneself, can be seen as an extreme form of the cultivation of eccentric identities and behaviors in modern society, as earlier noted in the works of Balzac and Simmel. But in its origins, Gelli and other duel investigators emphasized, the duel was a horribly violent, if highly ritualized act of self-appropriated "judicial combat."[32] In the earliest forms of dueling, the individual initiating the challenge would throw a glove to the ground, to be retrieved by the other combatant. Oaths were sworn to an impartial judge, a meal was shared, and arms were chosen. Then, with the *padrini*, or "seconds," attending to each combatant, the duelists were stripped, shaved, and oiled before entering an enclosed *campo*, or field, guarded by soldiers. The duelists then knelt, facing each other with arms crossed and hands clenched, swearing to "Truth" and affirming that neither had in any way attempted to cast spells or sorcery over the other. Relatives and friends, except for the *padrini*, were ordered to leave, and at the announcement "Let the good men go!" ("Lasciate andare i buoni uomini") the actual duel began. Uninhibited, vicious combat continued until either death or debilitating injury left one opponent incapacitated. Corpses of fallen duelists were routinely burned, while the dying injured were often hanged, conforming to ancient rituals with regard to successful or attempted suicides.[33]

Among contemporary commentators, Gelli and Tagliabue especially emphasized the historical development of the duel from the ninth century to their own time. Tagliabue argued that the European duel emerged a thousand years before his own time as an officially recognized act of "judicial combat," because of three major conditions:

> 1. A savage independence and freedom sustained in the shadow of crude and unformed government; 2. A badly defined sense of honor, founded on false and imperfect notions of valor, military prowess, and glorification of weapons; and 3. A blind superstition, which interpreted the result of combat as divine testimony determining rights and innocence.[34]

Tagliabue also reminded his readers of the Church's centuries-old condemnation of dueling, dating at least to the ninth-century Pope Nicholas I. Ecclesiastical letters and councils condemning the duel from the early Middle Ages to the Counter-Reformation of the 1500s and 1600s are also cited.[35] *Civiltà Cattolica* also argued that the Church had for centuries condemned dueling, even as any number of types of torture and "trial by ordeal" were practiced with papal approval.[36] In modern times, *Civiltà Cattolica* reminded its readers, Pio Nono (Pius IX) had in 1869 announced that all duelists and their accomplices were subject to automatic excommunication.[37] More recently, Pope Leo XIII had reaffirmed the Church's condemnation of dueling in his 1891 letter, *De prava duellorum consuetudine*, to the bishops of Germany and Austria where, as previously noted, the duel was both a serious problem and a college fraternity fad.[38]

As the writers at *Civiltà Cattolica* noted, duel apologists and those who argued against its criminalization had historically invoked the principle "*volenti non fit iniuria*," roughly translated as "consenting individuals are not harmed."[39] This formulation of the duel problem resembled classically Stoic approaches to suicide, as summed up in the phrase, "*Mori licet cui vivere non placuit*," or "Death is permitted for those whose life is not satisfying."[40]   Tagliabue cites Thomas Hobbes's and other classical thinkers' defense of the duel as a regrettable but "honorable" act of courage. The great champion of individual liberties Jeremy Bentham, Tagliabue notes, called dueling an absurd ritual but then wrote an extensive defense of one's right to engage in the practice. And Cesare Beccaria, Tagliabue reminds his readers, had argued that only the individual whose dishonorable actions gave rise to the duel in the first place should be liable for legal punishment.[41]

Most contemporary Italian critics of the duel agreed with Gelli's notion of the duel as "one of those social plagues which are not cured with force, but rather with persuasion."[42]   The statesman Massimo d'Azeglio—who, it will be remembered, famously commented that once Italy was united, it would be necessary to make Italians—took the same position:

> Unfortunately, the duel is rooted in that sentiment which the human heart has the most difficulty getting rid of: vanity. Vanity needs applause. And so, the remedy lies with the public spirit. Lacking applause, the duel will disappear.[43]

Tagliabue confronted this claim for the need of public approbation of the duel:

> A crime is not just intrinsically immoral but also must be recognized as such by public opinion, which regulates morality and dispenses reputation and shame. Now, as much as public opinion disapproves of the duel, it also imposes it as essential for the man of honor. Therefore, that which is necessary and inevitable cannot constitute a crime. So, others conclude that no law, whether of the nation, the crown, of wealth, or of life, should stand in the way of honor.[44]

Tagliabue disagreed with this position, arguing that dueling should be treated as pre-meditated murder freely engaged in by men whose actions should not be determined or forgiven by the force of public opinion. Without confronting the developing understanding of the duel as indirect suicide, Tagliabue asserted that the best protection from the perils of the duel was for men of honor to lead honest, open lives, free of "the specter of aberration."[45]

Although an official Italian section of the International League Against the Duel was not formed until December 21, 1902, early duel observers who subscribed to the "social plague" thesis had since 1868 sought to introduce voluntary guidelines and establish extra-judicial courts of honor to deal with the duel. These independent courts and their juries would be made up of honorable gentlemen, many of whom themselves had engaged in the duel. They would hear cases of defamation and regulate the duel in the hopes of reducing its frequency when possible while ensuring that those duels, which could not be avoided adhered to established chivalric codes.[46]

It should be noted that self-regulation, and not total abolition, of the duel was the primary goal of these groups. This was the source of much debate at the first International Congress Against the Duel, at Budapest in June 1908. The Italians were particularly active in such discussions.[47] Such proposals by duel advocates for non-criminalization were based in a profound belief in the indelible honor of gentlemen, and of their right as a social class to regulate their own disputes. Such advocates were also possessed of a deep, though not always stated, assumption that the duel was in its own honorable way, an acceptable suicidal act. Writing in 1880, the duel advocate Nicola Modugno echoed the more clinical sociological analyses of the duel as "indirect suicide," when he argued:

> Even those who declare themselves theoretically against the duel are, if they find themselves in life's unfortunate situations, nonetheless drawn into combat, content to end an unhappy existence on the field or to destroy whoever was the cause of their misery, instead of continuing an insufferable life, burdened with shame and ridicule.[48]

From a strictly social point of view, most proponents of the "courts of honor" also did not believe it was possible, or even advisable, to fully eradicate the duel. Taking a position which directly paralleled the contemporary belief that there existed an inverse ratio between suicide and homicide, advocates of "courts of honor" argued that there was also such a relationship between dueling and murder. Dueling, like suicide, was thought to serve as a kind of social "safety valve" which channeled violent behavior away from being taken out on society at large, into the limited realm of the immediate individuals involved.

In his 1888 book *Corte d'Onore*, which advocated the establishment of such "courts of honor" and delineated their procedures, Gelli asserted:

> It is axiomatic that the suppression of the duel would cause the number of murders to increase dramatically. This is true given the fact that hatred and rancor, if they do not find a chivalric and honorable way to release themselves, would burst out even more savagely and without doubt let loose in horrible excess, if not in treacherous violence of unequal or ambushed combat.[49]

Nicola Modugno went even further, arguing that the formal, chivalric structure of the duel had in some cases led to a resolution of conflict and flowering of male friendship even in the midst of near-mortal combat. Citing an account of one such experience in the memoirs of the 16th-century courtier Pierre Brantome, Modugno tells the following story:

> Two Roman soldiers, who for reasons of offenses exchanged between the two, challenged each other to a duel. But just as one of the two had been disarmed and was in the hands of the other, his opponent—not wanting to take unfair advantage of this victory—embraced and kissed him. And from that moment they remained the closest of friends.[50]

Given this complicated history of the duel and the various schools of thought which either supported or abhorred the practice, it should not be surprising that as the Italian parliament debated the so-called Zanardelli reforms of its first unitary penal code, it was said that the duel constituted "the most arduous and delicate problem in modern legislation."[51] Zanardelli himself forthrightly condemned the duel as a class-based affront to the authority of the state:

> Everything which is uncivil, wrong, and violent in the duel stems from a tradition of contempt toward the law, toward justice, and toward the sovereignty of the nation, by those who believe they may claim for themselves the right to wound or kill with impunity.[52]

Zanardelli and his winning side in the parliamentary debate over dueling also condemned the proposed courts of honor as a caste-based assault on the state's unique authority to judge and adjudicate conflict.[53] As Crivellari and other secular critics, and their cleric colleagues at *Civiltà Cattolica*, pointedly observed, the duel under Italy's new penal code of 1889 was thus classified not as a "crime against persons," but as a "crime against the administration of justice."[54] In this way, the duel was legally defined neither as akin to murder, which would have carried severe punishment, nor as akin to suicide, which carried no penalty. It could be argued that the lack of a legal linkage of the duel to homicide indicates how strongly held was the belief that dueling was in fact a form of indirect suicide. And just as suicide had once been illegal in civil law, on the technicality that no one had the right to deprive society of one's life and labors, the duel was condemned not so much for its violence against individuals but rather for its arrogant presumptions in depriving the state of its exclusive right to pass judgment in civil and criminal disputes.

Interestingly, the previously existing Sardinian and Tuscan Codes had defined the duel as a "crime against persons," even as such laws continued to represent rape, for example, as crimes against the honor of families and relatives of the victim.[55] The Sardinian code did recognize the explicit interest of the state in these matters, however, by its claim that the laws governing dueling applied even to duels fought outside its territorial boundaries if those duels had been provoked or arranged on land within its jurisdiction.[56]

The designation of the duel as a "crime against persons" did not mean that death resulting from a duel was considered on the same level as outright murder. Just as there were degrees of homicide written into law, causing another person's death in a duel was ranked at the low end of criminal culpability and punishment. Writing of the pre-Zanardelli laws on death resulting from dueling in effect across most of Italy, Alberto Franco Nunes disapprovingly noted in 1865:

> The Italian code on this matter is maybe the mildest known, since it punishes such a homicide with a jail term of not less than one year and a fine of not more than a thousand lire.[57]

By contrast, Nunes noted that in certain jurisdictions of the United States, dueling was a capital offense; and in Portugal, duelists could have their property confiscated and were liable to internal exile. Nunes also disagreed with the pre-Zanardelli dueling codes' assignation of greater culpability to the duelist who "provoked the altercation which gave rise to the duel." Instead, he argued that both duelists should receive similar penalties, including the aggrieved challenger, "in order to push him to avail himself of the protection of the law against such offense."[58] Nunes was equally critical of the pre-Zanardelli code's treatment of the *padrini*, or "seconds," who observed and facilitated the duel, because the law "did not consider them accomplices, except if they had instigated the duel."[59]

By contrast, the Zanardelli provisions stiffened penalties for every level of duel activity, while not likening the duel to murder itself.[60] A simple challenge to duel, even if not carried out, was subject to a fine of up to five hundred lire. If such a challenger was the cause of the scandalous situation leading to the duel challenge, he could be jailed for up to two months, even if the duel did not finally occur. Whoever accepted a duel challenge, even if it eventually did not take place, faced a fine of from one hundred to 1,500 lire.[61]

If the duel did take place, fines were increased. The simple use of arms in a duel, even if no injury resulted, merited jail time of up to two months. That person of the two duelists determined to have been the "unjust cause" of the duel was subject to jail time of from 15 days to four months.[62] In this incremental manner, all aspects and possible outcomes of the duel carried more serious penalties than had previously been the case. But even being found guilty of killing another person in a duel carried a mild penalty of a jail term ranging from just six months to five years.[63] Even these light prison sentences were subject to reduction by as much as a third if the convicted duelist who caused the death of another could show that he had been "induced to duel because of serious insult or affront."[64]

Further heightening the prevailing definition of the duel as more legally akin to suicide than to homicide was the provision of article 243 which provided for prosecution under homicide statutes of any alleged duelist who did not follow traditional dueling rules and protocol. Thus, failure to engage *padrini*, or "seconds," and witnesses in the challenge phase and in the duel itself, and the use of any weapon other than sabers, swords, and pistols disqualified such combat as a duel, remanding surviving participants to the homicide courts.[65] In all duel cases, *padrini* and witnesses were liable to varying fines of up to one thousand lire. Successful intervention stopping a duel set such *padrini* free of punishment for their previous violation in setting up the event.[66] Any individual who stood in for a previously announced duelist, serving as a surrogate combatant, was subject to an increase in the applicable fines and jail time by as much as one half. But this penalty increase did not apply if the stand-in was an immediate relative of the duelist, or if he was one of the *padrini* who was traditionally expected to fight in the last minute absence of his duelist friend.[67]

Interestingly, the new law reserved most serious punishment for those who would manipulate others into duel situations. The mere attempt to embarrass someone publicly with the charge that they had not accepted an honorable challenge to a duel or that they had recoiled from properly challenging someone else to a duel, could carry a jail term ranging from one month to a year.[68] The most serious punishments of all were reserved for anyone found to have provoked, challenged, or participated in a duel for the purposes of financial gain. Such dishonorable persons were subject to prison terms ranging from three to 15 years.[69]

The Zanardelli provisions on the duel were a difficult compromise struck between strict abolitionists and those who found value in the duel. As late as 1898, with the duel not brought fully under control a decade after the Zanardelli reforms went into effect, unsuccessful proposals were still being made in parliament to establish the much-touted courts of honor.[70] In these continuing debates, the duel was not only still defended as a necessary cultural safety valve, but also extolled, in the words of the parliamentary deputy Silvio Venturi, as a "morally elevated" act.[71] Venturi went so far as to argue that the institution of the duel and the social stratification which guaranteed its place of privilege beyond the normal structures of society and law, actually served as an incentive for the lower classes to improve their lot, in hopes of "attaining such glorious and exalted status."[72]

This perceived connection of violence, personal fulfillment, and social status, was also linked by contemporary writers to war and Italian national identity. In his 1880 book on dueling, Nicola Modugno had commented on Luigi Settembrini's belief:

> To train oneself in the use of arms and to engage in dueling was a commendable system of civil education for the nation, because it prepared young people to defiantly challenge the dangers of destiny and of war, assuring the fatherland of a bold, courageous, and strong youth.[73]

As was seen in the case of *Jacopo Ortis*, suicide and Italian national identity had for at least a century maintained a curious, if much criticized, relationship. A variation on such sentiments, in which war replaced suicide, and even the duel, as the emblematic experience of national identity had become increasingly common as Italy entered the new century. Italy's most important political-literary journals—*Hermes, Leonardo, Il Regno,* and *La Voce*—regularly published celebrations of war not only as a means of asserting Italian territorial and catch-up colonialist claims, but also as a personal and collective way of transforming life into something heroic beyond everyday existence. At the same time, the duel itself became an object of ridicule in the articles of these reviews. Writing in *La Voce* in 1909, for example, Luigi Ambrosini mockingly reflected earlier analyses of the duel as an anachronistic holdover of a bygone era, asserting ironically:

The duel is a doubly bourgeois institution, for the duelists and for the spectators. It is so basely bourgeois, so devoid of any chivalric meaning, so absent of any military sentiment, that in the army itself, the duel is on the verge of rapidly disappearing.[74]

The nationalist Enrico Corradini was among the most outspoken of Italians in this period who were fascinated with war as a cleansing experience. Commenting on the Russo-Japanese war of 1904, in which Italy had no real interest and played no part, Corradini remarked:

I have some friends who are stained and polluted by all of the perversions of non-violent civilization; nonetheless, most of these friends are taken up with the charms of war; they feel the aesthetic sensations of the distant spectacle among unleashed forces; they admire the Japanese ships, which search and attack the enemy night and day. These friends have—without knowing so—become men again, true to their natural state.[75]

Similarly, in his appropriately titled *The Race to Death*, the nationalist Marcello Taddei declared himself to be descended from "a distant people who lived off of war and who had ascetics as judges, and who were great because of their warriors."[76] The most notorious of so many thousands of such contemporary pronouncements came in 1909 when the self-proclaimed Futurists, most outspokenly led by Filippo Tommaso Marinetti, declared that war was "the world's only hygiene."[77] In both their writings and infamous *Serate futuriste* (Futurist Evenings) of mock riot and performance mayhem, the Futurists expressed "scorn for woman" while glorifying the all-male world of combat in clinically pornographic, anatomically female terms:

See the furious coitus of war, gigantic vulva stirred by the friction of courage, shapeless vulva that spreads to offer itself to the terrific spasm of final victory.[78]

While this study has attempted to limit itself to a strictly empirical overview of Italian suicide from 1860 to 1915—placing contemporary Italian voices up front, to be heard on their own terms—further investigation of the possible links between such glorification of war and the suicidal impulse during these years is warranted. Is there evidence in this period of Italian history, for example, to show that war—like dueling—had become a kind of "indirect suicide?" Did this indirect suicide in the name of national honor serve as a kind of "indirect duel," conferring honorable status not just to the elites, but also to the masses of the new Italian society, many of whom still did not even enjoy the right to vote? Did a homoerotic reality of everyday life in the wars of national liberation contribute to the simultaneously feminized and misogynistic tone of contemporary Italian war rhetoric? And what role did women play in this increasingly bellicose drama?

These legitimate questions cannot be definitively examined in this current, brief study of suicide. Further investigations of such issues would have to take into account contemporary Italy's strong but fractured, and ultimately ineffectual, pacifist movement.[79] However, the question of whether a socio-cultural connection links suicide, the duel, and war becomes all the more compelling when one observes accounts by the contemporary writer Renato Serra, among others, of the wildly popular demonstrations and departures for war against the aging Ottoman Empire, in Italy's successful colonialist effort to take Libya in 1911.[80] "How could it be?" Serra asks:

> It is certainly a beautiful spectacle. Ten years ago no one could have dreamed it. The sound of it all is fake. But one can't say that in some way the whole thing isn't sincere.[81]

Serra was saddened and astonished that so many Italian boys and young men "go off to be a soldier so happily, and read the papers, exalting combat."[82] But Serra's critical analysis of the appeal of war was tempered by a resignation to the apparently greater, anthropological truths of human existence in the history of Italian national existence. Lamenting the behavior of his compatriots, Serra acceded to their fate:

> These people who no longer want to know anything of humanitarianism, of internationalism, of solidarity, of all the material and petty fetishes of the last generation, have not overcome this crisis with intelligence. But it must also be said that they are not just obeying the current fashion. These people obey history, in which nothing gets lost.[83]

Serra's observations apply equally to the riotous days leading up to Italy's belated entry into World War I, in May 1915. Marauding hordes of young men took to the streets throughout the new nation and stormed the parliament in Rome during the so-called "radiant days of May," successfully demanding to join the year-old European battle, switching sides from Germany and a never-loved Austria, to fight on the side of England, Russia, and France.[84] A further examination of such demand for war on the part of a significant segment of the documentably, suicidal male population in Italy during this period would have to take into account Mario Morasso's contemporary view that as "stress will have become the defining characteristic of modern life," war was becoming sport, "the most noble sport, the most fervent, the most demanded, the first of all sports, as it was for patrician Rome and the medieval knight."[85]

If it may seem that this deliberately limited and tersely empirical history of suicide in Italy ends not so much with final conclusions as with further questions, it is hoped that this is true because the questions could not have been asked in the absence of the evidence heretofore given. The German-Jewish aesthete Walter Benjamin, who in 1940 killed himself in flight, under threat of arrest at the fascist-occupied, French-Spanish border, is renowned for his comment against the debilitating aspects of the most disruptive tendencies of modern life and the glorification of such social rupture as expressed in Marinetti's Futurist credo:

> Its self-alienation has reached such a degree that it can experience its own destruction as an aesthetic pleasure of the first order.[86]

The history of Futurist agitation for social unrest and war is another book. This book must confine itself more strictly to the history of suicide in Italy from 1860 to 1915, on its own terms and without regard to the issues this book suggests ought to in the future be covered. So, rather than ending this history of suicide in Italy at the last turn of the century on a conjectural, philosophical note, it seems only right to let this story tell its own end, with an excerpt from a letter from a soldier writing home on December 8, 1915 from the front of the Great War. He gets the last word:

> Grenades, bombs, shrapnel, poison gas, rifle-fire, and the rest, which continually delight us. It's even pretty here; the beauty lies in the danger. If I had to die, I would die happily as I have seen die so many good companions and friends. But don't get upset over what I'm saying: these words are neither a bad wish nor anything else. They are just words that describe what could happen, but not what necessarily will happen.[87]

Notes

[1]See chapter two, pp. 38–40: Ferri (notes 124–26, 131,132); Sighele (note 127); Altavilla (notes 128, 129); J.C. de Breyne (note 130).
[2] Gabriel Tarde, in Ferri, *Omicidio-suicidio*, p. 146.

3 Tarde, in Ferri, *Omicidio-suicidio*, p. 147.

4 Lombroso, *Crime*, p. 417.

5 Ferri, *Omicidio-suicidio*, p. 67.

6 *Nuova Antologia*, Filippo Crispolti, *"L'Italia e il moto internazionale contro il duello,"* (Nov.-Dec., 1902), pp. 135–47; and R. Garofolo, *"Il codice per i galantuomini,"* (Jan.-Feb., 1902), pp. 686–92. Among the hundreds of books on the duel in this period (and before and after), many privately published, see Fabio Albergati, *Trattato del modo di ridurre a pace l'inimicizie private* (Rome: Dragondelli, 1664); Matteo Liberatore, *Del diritto sulla vita per quel che concerne il suicidio, il duello, la pena di morte* (Naples, 1845); Carlo Ravizza, *Il suicidio, il sacrificio della vita, e il duello* (Milan, 1849); Pietro Ellero, *Del Duello* (Modena, 1865); Alberto Franco Nunes, *Del duello e dei mezzi più opportuni a bandirlo dalla società* (Turin: Unione tipografica editrice, 1865); Antonio Tagliabue, *Il duello* (Milan, 1867); Nicola Modugno, *Pena capitale e duello* (Naples, 1869) and *Il duello* (Bari, 1880); Paolo Fambri, *La giurisprudenza del duello* (Florence, 1869); Michelangelo Accampo, *Il duello e la moderna civiltà* (Naples, 1870); Giulio Crivellari, *Il duello nella dottrina e nella giurisprudenza* (Turin, 1884); Jacopo Gelli, *Il duello nella storia della giurisprudenza e pratica italiana* (Florence: Loescher e Seeber, 1886); Luigi Barbasetti, *Codice cavalleresco* (Milan: Gattinoni, 1898); Carlo Lessona, *Il duello nei nuovi studi e nelle nuove idee* (Pisa: editore Spoerri, 1901); Emilio Federici, *Guerra al duello* (Venice: tipografia Emiliana, 1903); Angelo Coelli, *Il duello attraverso i secoli* (Milan: Libreria editrice nazionale, 1904); Jacopo Nicoletti, *Del duello civile e militare ed argomenti atti a distruggerlo* (Florence: tipografia Nazionale, 1904); Antonio Russo-Ajello, *Il duello secondo i principii, la dottrina, la legislazione* (Città di Castello, 1906); C. Lovati, *Il duello: conversazioni di un avvocato* (Milan, 1908); Pasquale Arecca, *Contro il duello* (Campobasso, 1917); Giulio da Re, *Vicende giuridiche e storiche del duello* (Milan: Editrice Libraria, 1921); Giuseppe Ettore, *Questioni d'onore* (Milan: Hoepli, 1928); Jacopo Gelli, *Duelli Celebri* (Milan: Hoepli, 1928); and, for the post-war Fascist period, Niccolo Molinini, *Il suicidio e il duello nella concezione fascista* (Bari, 1934).

7 Antonio Tagliabue, *Il Duello* (Milan: n.p., 1867), p. 79; and Tagliabue, *Il suicidio* (Milan: Croci, 1871).

8 Tagliabue, *Il Duello*, p. 12; p. 8 for competition sponsorship.

9 Tagliabue, *Il Duello*, p. 30.

10 Tagliabue, *Il Duello*, p. 30.

11 See, for example, *"I Moderni Iloti del Punto d'Onore,"* part I, *Civiltà Cattolica*, xv, vol. 6, June 1896, pp. 641–656, and part II, *Civiltà Cattolica*, xvi, vol. 7, June 1896, pp. 162–178; *"La Deformità Giuridica del Duello,"* *Civiltà Cattolica*, xvii, vol. 1, March 1898, pp. 678–691, p. 678 for the above quote; *"Il Duello a Montecitorio,"* *Civiltà Cattolica*, xvii, vol. 2, April 1898, pp. 257–267; *"L'Apologia di un Delitto,"* *Civiltà Cattolica*, xvii, vol. 2, May 1898, pp. 385–398. *Civiltà Cattolica* provided extensive coverage and commentary on duelling throughout the period under review, as well as in the years after World War I, when dueling enjoyed a brief revival. See, for example, the following *Civiltà Cattolica* citations: *"Mondo e Mondani Intorno ad un Duello"*, xvii, v. 9, Feb. 1900, p. 580; *"Lega internazionale contro il duello,"* xviii, v. 9, Jan. 1903, p. 230; *"Guerra al Duello,"* xviii, v. 12, Nov. 1903, pp. 451–459; *"La Lega Contro il Duello,"* v. 4, Oct. 1904, pp. 507–510, and note 5, p. 632; vol. 4, Nov. 1906, pp. 488–

491; *"Il Duello Secondo i Principii, La Dotttrina, La Legislazione,"* v. 2, May 1907, pp. 585–590; on military duels, Note 3, v. 4, Nov. 1908, pp. 492–93; on post-World War I revival of dueling, Nov. 1921, note 7, pp. 467–69; Oct. 1922, note 8, p. 176–179; Dec. 1922, note 7, p. 568.

[12] *"I Moderni Iloti del Punto d'Onore,"* Civiltà Cattolica, xvi, vol. 7, June 1896, p.164, citing *Atti del Ministero di agricoltura, industria, e commercio, "Cause di morte"* (Rome, 1896), n.p.

[13] *"La Deformità Giuridica del Duello,"* Civiltà Cattolica, xvii, vol. 1, March 1898, p. 678, citing Ministero di Agricoltura, industria, e commercio, *"Cause di morte"* (Rome, 1897), pp. LXVIII.

[14] Jacopo Gelli, *Duelli celebri* (Milan: Hoepli, 1928), p. 17; and Civiltà Cattolica, Nov. 1921, vol. 4, *"Cose Italiane,"* no. 7, p. 467.

[15] Gelli, *Duelli celebri*, p. 17.

[16] Gelli, *Il duello nella storia della giurisprudenza e nella pratica* (Florence: Loescher and Seeber, 1886) p. 27; and Angelo Coelli, *Il duello attraverso i secoli* (Milan: Libreria editrice nazionale, 1904), p. 95; Gelli, *Duelli celebri*, 1928, p. 17.

[17] Gelli, *Duelli celebri*, 1928, p. 18.

[18] Gelli, *Il duello nella storia*, 1886, p.22.

[19] Tagliabue, *Il duello* (1867), p. 71.

[20] Coelli, *Il duello attraverso i secoli* (1904), p. 97.

[21] On this general dynamic of bourgeois appropriation of aristocratic ritual and style from the French Revolution to World War I, see Arno Mayer, *The Persistence of the Old Regime: Europe to the Great War* (New York: Pantheon, 1981).

[22] Gelli, *Duelli celebri* (1928), p. 16.

[23] *"La Deformità Giuridica del Duello,"* Civiltà Cattolica, xvi, vol. I, March 1898, p. 679.

[24] *"I Moderni Iloti del Punto d'Onore,"* Civiltà Cattolica, xv, vol. vi, June 1896, p. 642, naming dueling parliamentary deputies Barzilai, Casale, Cavalotti, Coaianni, Gaetani di Laurenzana, Ginori, Imbriani-Poerio, Luzzatto, Mocenni, Modestino, Muratori, Vendemini.

[25] *"La Deformità Giuridica del Duello,"* Civiltà Cattolica, xvii, vol. I, March, 1898, p. 678, citing the Rome daily *Il Messaggero*, March 7, 1898.

[26] *"L'Apologia di un Delitto,"* Civiltà Cattolica, xvii, vol. 2, May 1898, p. 398.

[27] Gelli, *Il duello* (1886), p. 46.

[28] Gelli, *Il duello* (1886), p. 46.

[29] Gelli, *Il duello* (1886), p. 98.

[30] On the Germanic duel tradition see Nicola Modugno, *Il duello* (Bari, 1880), pp. 27–28; Ute Frevert, "Bourgeois honor: Middle-class duellists in Germany," in David Blackbourne and Richard Evans, *The German Bourgeoisie: Essays on the Social History of the German Middle Class from the Late Eighteenth to the Twentieth Century* (London: Routledge, 1991), pp. 255–92; V.G. Kiernan, *The Duel in European History: Honor and the Reign of Aristocracy* (Oxford: Oxford University Press, 1988); Francois Billacois, *The Duel: Its Rise and Fall in Early Modern France* (New Haven: Yale University Press, 1990); and Kevin McAleer, *Dueling: The Cult of Honor in Fin-de-Siècle Germany* (Princeton: Princeton University Press, 1994).

[31] Gelli, *Il duello* (1886), p. 99.

[32] Gelli, *Il duello* (1886), p. 9.

[33] Gelli, *Il duello* (1886), p. 9.

[34] Tagliabue, *Il duello*, p. 21.

[35] Tagliabue, *Il duello*, p. 60.

[36] *"I Moderni Iloti del Punto d'Onore,"* Civiltà Cattolica, xvi, vol. 7, June 1896, p. 176, note 1.

[37] *"I Moderni Iloti del Punto d'Onore,"* Civiltà Cattolica, xvi, vol. 7, June 1896, p. 176, citing Pius IX's Apostolic Bull, *Apostolicae Sedis*, October 10, 1869.

[38] *"I Moderni Iloti del Punto d'Onore,"* Civiltà Cattolica, xvi, vol. 7, June 1896, p. 176, 178; *"La Deformità Giuridica del Duello,"* Civiltà Cattolica, xvii, vol. 1, March 1898, p. 691. Also cited in McAleer, *Dueling* (1994), p. 152–53. Civiltà Cattolica's contemporary account contradicts McAleer's sources, which he cites as confirming only a "threat" of excommunication for duelists and their accomplices.

[39] *"La Deformità Giuridica del Duello,"* Civiltà Cattolica, xvii, vol. I, March 1898, p. 689.

[40] Luigi, Previti, *"Il Suicidio,"* Civiltà Cattolica, xviii, vol. I, Feb. 1886, p. 516.

[41] Tagliabue, *Il Duello* (1867), p. 19.

[42] Gelli, *Il Duello* (1886), p. 21.

[43] Massimo d'Azeglio, *I miei Ricordi* (Florence, 1867), vol. I, p. 223, cited in *"I Moderni Iloti del Punto d'Onore,"* Civiltà Cattolica, xv, vol. VI, June 1896, p. 644.

[44] Tagliabue, *Il Duello* (1867), p. 52.

[45] Tagliabue, *Il Duello* (1867), p. 57.

[46] On the founding of the Italian League Against the Duel, see Civiltà Cattolica, *"Cronaca,"* note 4, xviii, vol. 9, Jan. 1903, p. 230. On the "court of honor" movement's first action in 1868, see *"I Moderni Iloti del Punto d'Onore,"* Civiltà Cattolica, xvi, vol. vii, June 1896, p. 171; and *"Il Duello a Montecitorio,"* Civiltà Cattolica, xvii, vol. II, April, 1898, p. 260, note 2, citing Paolo Fambri, *La giurisprudenza del duello* (Florence, 1869), pp. 192–93.

[47] See *Compte Rendu du Ier Congres International Contre Le Duel*, June 4–6 (Budapest: Edition de la Ligue Hongroise Contre le Duel, 1908).

[48] Nicola Modugno, *Il Duello* (1880), p. 72.

[49] Gelli, *Corte d'Onore permanente in Firenze* (Florence: De Angelis, 1888), p. 5.

[50] Modugno, *Il Duello* (1880), p. 19.

[51] Crivellari, *Il Codice* (1890), p. CCLXXVIII.

[52] *"I Moderni Iloti del Punto d'Onore,"* Civiltà Cattolica, xvi, vol. VII, June 1896, p. 167, citing Zanardelli's Ministry of Justice summary report on the duel to the king, *Relazione a S.M. del Ministro Guardasigilli* (Naples, 1890), p. 149.

[53] *"Il Duello a Montecitorio,"* Civiltà Cattolica, xvii, vol. II, April 1898, p. 262, citing *"Relazione"* (Naples, 1890), p. 149, p. 264 of same Civiltà Cattolica article.

[54] Crivellari, *Il Codice* (1889), Libro II, Titolo IX, *"Dei delitti contro l'Amministrazione della giustizia,"* pp. 88–89, note 9; and *"Il Duello a Montecitorio,"* Civiltà Cattolica, p. xvii, vol. II, April 1898, pp. 263–264.

[55] Crivellari, *Codice penale* (1889), p. 88, citing *Codice toscano*, articles 340–350; and Codice sardo, articles 589–595.

[56] Crivellari, *Codice penale* (1889), p. 89, citing article 595.

[57] Alberto Franco Nunes, *Del duello e dei mezzi più opportuni a bandirlo dalla società* (Turin: Unione tipografica editrice, 1865), p. 98.

[58] Nunes, *Del duello* (1865), p. 99, 104.

[59] Nunes, *Del duello* (1865), p. 107.

[60] Crivellari, *Il Codice* (1889), p. 89; and Crivellari, *Il Codice* (1890), vol. 6, ed. Giovanni Suman (1895), articles 237–245, pp. 798–800, with additional voluminous commentary on parliamentary debate over dueling, pp. 801–951. Suman edited volumes 6-8 of this compendium after Crivellari's death.

[61] Crivellari (1889), article 237, p. 97; Suman (1895), p. 798.

[62] Crivellari (1889), article 238, p. 97; Suman (1895), p. 798.

[63] Crivellari (1889), article 239, p. 98; Suman (1895), p. 798.

[64] Crivellari (1889), article 240, p. 98; Suman (1895), p. 799.

[65] Crivellari (1889), article 243, p. 98; Suman (1895) p. 799.

[66] Crivellari (1889), article 241, p. 98; Suman (1895), p. 799.

[67] Crivellari (1889), article 242, p. 98; Suman (1895), p. 799.

[68] Crivellari (1889), article 244, p. 99; Suman (1895), p. 800.

[69] Crivellari (1889), article 245, p. 99; Suman (1895), p. 800.

[70] *"Il Duello a Montecitorio,"* *Civiltà Cattolica*, xvii, vol. II, April 1898, p. 257, note 1, and p. 260, citing parliamentary deputy De Martino's proposal of March 19, 1898.

[71] *L'Apologia di un Delitto*, *Civiltà Cattolica*, xvii, vol. II, May 1898, p. 385, citing parliamentary deputy Silvio Venturi's remarks of April 16, 1898.

[72] Venturi, *"L'Apologia di un Delitto,"* *Civiltà Cattolica*, xvii, vol. II, May 1898, p. 397.

[73] Nicola Modugno, *Il Duello* (1880), p. 26.

[74] Luigi Ambrosini, *"Noi che non ci battiamo,"* *La Voce*, Oct. 14, 1909, p. 451, and pp. 450–55.

[75] Enrico Corradini, *"La guerra,"* in *Il Regno*, vol. I, 1904, pp. 1–2, cited in Delia Castelnuovo Frigessi, *La cultura italiana del '900 attraverso le riviste* (Turin: Einaudi, 1970), p. 482.

[76] Marcello Taddei, *"La Corsa alla Morte,"* in *Hermes*, vol. V, 1904, pp. 211–222, repr. in Frigessi, *La cultura* (1970), pp. 414–26; this quote, p. 420.

[77] F.T. Marinetti, "Founding Manifesto of Futurism," first published in *Le Figaro*, Feb. 20, 1909, p. 1; repr. in R.W. Flint, ed., *Let's Murder the Moonshine: Selected Writings of F.T. Marinetti* (Los Angeles: Sun & Moon Classics, 1991), p. 50.

[78] Marinetti, *"Let's Murder the Moonshine,"* April 1909, in Flint, 1991, *Let's Murder*, p. 61.

[79] See Sandi Cooper, *Patriotic Pacifism: Waging War on War in Europe, 1815–1914* (New York: Oxford University Press, 1991).

[80] Renato Serra, *"Partenza di un gruppo di soldati per la Libia,"* 1912, repr. in Mario Isnenghi, ed., Renato Serra, *Scritti letterari, morali e politici: saggi e articoli dal 1900 al 1915* (Turin: Einaudi, 1974), pp. 277–288.

[81] Serra, *Partenza*, pp. 279–280.

[82] Serra, *Partenza*, p. 282–83.

[83] Serra, *Partenza*, p. 283.

[84] See Brunello Vigezzi, *"Le radiose giornate del maggio 1915"*, in Vigezzi, *Da Giolitti a Salandra* (Florence: Vallecchi, 1969), pp. 111–200 and pp. 321–401.

[85] Mario Morasso, *La nuova guerra: armi, combattimenti, battaglie* (Milan: Treves, 1914), p. 189.

[86] Walter Benjamin, "The Work of Art in the Age of Mechanical Reproduction," (1936), in Hannah Arendt, ed., *Illuminations* (New York: Schocken Books, 1978), p. 242.

[87] Adolfo Omodeo, *Momenti della vita di guerra: Dai diari e dalle lettere dei caduti, 1915–1918* (Turin: Einaudi, 1968), p. 48.

Conclusion

In his magisterial study *Crowds and Power*, Elias Canetti remarks that Italians are fortunate because "the attempt to impose a false crowd symbol on Italy was a failure."[1] Canetti's diagnosis of the Italian national character refers to the period from national unification to World War I, as well as to the two-decade *ventennio* of Fascism from 1922–44 and beyond.

Canetti was happy to report that neither the nineteenth-century Liberal nor twentieth-century Fascist regimes had succeeded in forcing a "national feeling" onto a people whose collective identity had been "paralyzed" from the time of national unification. Canetti's optimism, stemming from the failure of the Italian people to fully embrace Fascism, however, was subdued by his realistic assessment of the weaknesses of democratic Italian society and the paralytic skepticism of so many citizens against participating fully in the affairs of the post-Fascist, democratic state.

By Canetti's account, history had played a "spiteful trick" on Italy. The unity born of the common struggle to unite as one country a diverse conglomeration of peoples living from Sicily to the Alps had given way to "the difficulty a nation has in visualizing itself when all its cities are haunted by greater memories."[2] Italians saddled with the literal remnants and historical memory of the First Rome of the Caesars and the Second Rome of the Popes—not to mention the fierce traditions of other regional identities— were, by Canetti's account, hostage to a localized history and particularized memory, which undermined the potential vigor of the new democratic, secular, and pan-Italian Third Rome.

This struggling Third Rome at the head of an old and tired Italy fit for not much more than romantic tourists and angry, home-grown Futurists, trying to catch up with the rest of its modern European rivals, was weighted with what the contemporary art historian Alois Riegl referred to as the clash between age value, historical value, and intentional commemorative value.

Age value appreciates the past for itself, while historical value singles out one moment in the developmental continuum of the past and places it before our eyes as if it belonged to the present. Intentional commemorative value aims to preserve a monument in the consciousness of later generations, and therefore to remain alive and present in perpetuity.[3]

A more detailed study of Rome and the building of monuments in the Liberal and Fascist periods would reveal the manner in which the conflict of Riegl's three aspects of art conservancy played out in the civic and architectural debate over the legacy of the three Romes. For the purposes of this study of suicide in this period of Italian history, however, it should be sufficient to note, as Canetti has said:

> Before Italy had won its unity, things were far clearer in the minds of its people. As soon as the parasitic enemy had been driven out, the dismembered body would be pieced together again and would feel and act as a single organism.[4]

Or would it? As Canetti notes: "Between these two Romes the national feeling of modern Italy was, as it were, paralyzed." The anonymous soldier ready to die in battle in World War I was also paralyzed and full of civic ambition. He, finally, again, gets the last word:

> Grenades, bombs, shrapnel, poison gas, rifle-fire, and the rest, which continually delight us. It's even pretty here; the beauty lies in the danger. If I had to die, I would die happily as I have seen die so many good companions and friends. But don't get upset over what I'm saying: these words are neither a bad wish nor anything else. They are just words that describe what could happen, but not what necessarily will happen.[5]

Notes

[1] Elias Canetti, *Crowds and Power* (New York: Farrar Straus Giroux, 1984), p. 178; orig. pub. *Masse und Macht* (Hamburg: Classen Verlag, 1960).
[2] Canetti, p. 177.
[3] Alois Riegl, "The Modern Cult of Monuments: Its Character and Its Origin," 1903, in Kurt W. Forster, ed., *Monument/Memory, Oppositions*, Fall 1982, no. 25 (New York: Institute for Architecture and Urban Studies/Rizzoli), pp. 21–51.
[4] Canetti, *Crowds and Power*, p. 177
[5] Adolfo Omodeo, *Momenti della vita di Guerra: Dai diari e dalle lettere dei caduti, 1915–1918* (Turin: Einaudi, 1968), p. 48.

Bibliography

Primary sources

Newspapers

Il Corriere della Sera (Milan)
Il Gazzettino (Venice, Treviso editions)
Il Resto del Carlino (Bologna)
La Gazzetta di Mantova (Mantua)
La Gazzetta Ferrarese (Ferrara)
La Nazione (Florence)
La Provincia di Como (Como)
La Stampa (Turin)

Parliamentary and organizational records

Aspetti della politica liberale (Rome: Chamber of Deputies, 1974).

Compte Rendu du Ier Congres International Contre le Duel (Budapest: Ligue Nationale Hongroise Contre le Duel, 1908).

Journals

Archivio di Psichiatria (Turin).
Civiltà Cattolica (Rome).
Il Regno (Florence).
L'Artista Moderno (Rome).
La Voce (Florence).
Lacerba (Florence).
Leonardo (Florence).
Novissima (Rome).
Nuova Antologia (Rome).

Books

Accampo, Michelangelo, *Il duello e la moderna civiltà* (Naples, 1870).

Acciaresi, Primo, *Giuseppe Sacconi e l'opera sua massima: cronaca dei lavori del monumento nazionale a Vittorio Emanuele* (Rome: Tipografia dell'unione editrice, 1911).

Adams, Henry, *The Education of Henry Adams* (New York: 1897).

Albergati, Fabio, *Trattato del modo di ridurre a pace l'inimicitie private* (Rome: Dragonelli, 1664).

Altavilla, Enrico, *La psicologia del suicidio: intuizioni psicologiche, documentazioni artistiche* (Naples: Perrella, 1910).

Antonini, G., and Cognetti de Martis, L., *Vittorio Alfieri: studi psicopatologici* (Turin: Bocca, 1898).

Arecca, Pasquale, *Contro il duello* (Campobasso, 1917).

Aymard, Marcel, *Le duel et la loi en France et à l'etranger* (Paris: Rousseau, 1907).

Bacelli, Alfredo, *Nell'Ombra dei Vinti* (Turin: Tipografia editrice nazionale, 1909).

Bailo, Luigi, *Guida della Città di Treviso* (1872; Treviso: Canova, 1978).

Balzac, Honoré de, *History of the Thirteen* (London: Penguin Books, 1978; orig. *Histoire des Treize*, Paris, 1833-35).

Barbasetti, Luigi, *Codice cavalleresco* (Milan: Gattinoni, 1898).

Baudelaire, Charles, *Paris Spleen* (Paris, 1869; New York: New Directions, 1947).

Beccaria, Cesare, *Dei delitti e delle pene* (Milan, 1764).

Bloch, Ivan, *La vita sessuale dei nostri tempi* (Turin: Bocca, 1912).

Bonomelli, Geremia, *Il suicidio* (Rome, 1910).

Bonomi, Serafino, *Del suicidio in Italia* (Milan: Vallardi, 1878).

Buonvino, Orazio, *Il giornalismo contemporaneo* (Palermo: Remo Sandron, 1906).

Cangiullo, Francesco, *Le serate futuriste: Romanzo storico vissuto* (Naples, 1930).

Capellanus, Andreas, *The Art of Courtly Love* (c.1186; New York: Columbia University Press, 1990).

Caponi, Giuseppe, *Il suicidio: studio etico-giuridico* (Genoa, 1913).

Castiglione, Baldassar, *Il libro del corteggiano* (Venice, 1528).

Coelli, Angelo, *Il duello attraverso i secoli* (Milan: Libreria editrice nazionale, 1904).

Comisso, Giovanni, *Giorni di Guerra* (1930; Milan: Longanesi, 1987).

Corradini, *Per la guerra d'Italia* (Rome: Società anonima, 1915).

Crescini, Vicenzo, *Per la questione delle corti d'amore* (Padua: Randi, 1891).

Crivellari, Giulio, *Il codice penale per il Regno d'Italia* (Turin: Unione tipografico-editrice, 1889).

————, *Il codice penale per il Regno d'Italia* (Turin: Unione tipografico editrice, 1890).

————, *Il duello nella dottrina e nella giurisprudenza* (Turin, 1884).

Croce, Benedetto, *Filosofia, poesia, storia* (Milan: Ricciardi, 1951).

————, *Storia d'Italia dal 1871 al 1915* (Bari: Laterza, 1928).

Curci, Carlo Maria, *Il suicidio studiato in sè e nelle sue cagioni* (Florence, 1876).

Da Re, Giulio, *Vicende giuridiche e storiche del duello* (Milan: Editrice Libraria, 1921).

De Breyne, *Du Suicide: considere aux points de vue philosophique, religieux, moral, et medical* (Paris: Rusand, 1847).

De Luna, Antonio, *Il suicidio nel diritto e nella vita sociale* (Rome, 1907).

De Mauro, Mauro, *Del suicidio e del concorso in esso riguardo al dritto di punire* (Catania: Bellini, 1876).

De Stefani, Alessandro, *Malati di Passione* (Milan: Baldini, 1922).

Deledda, Grazia, *Amori moderni* (Rome: Voghera, 1907).

Donne, John, *Biathanatos* (1644).

Durkheim, Emile, *Le suicide: Etude de sociologie* (Paris, 1897; New York: Free Press, 1951).

Eberhardt, Isabelle, *The Oblivion Seekers* (San Francisco: City Lights, 1982).

Ellero, Pietro, *Del Duello* (Modena, 1865).

———, *La tirannide borghese* (Bologna: Zanichelli, 1879).

Erasmus, *In Praise of Folly* (1509).

Ettore, Giuseppe, *Questioni d'onore* (Milan: Hoepli, 1928).

Fambri, Paolo, *La giurisprudenza del duello* (Florence, 1869).

Federici, Emilio, *Guerra al duello* (Venice: tipografia Emiliana, 1903).

Ferrrari, Paolo, *Il suicidio: Commedia in 5 atti* (Milan, 1878).

Ferri, Enrico, *I delinquenti nell'arte* (Genoa: Libreria moderna, 1901).

———, *Omicidio-suicidio: responsabilità giuridica* (Turin: Bocca, 1895).

———, and Fornasari di Verce, Ettore, *Il Marinaio Epilettico e la Delinquenza Militare* (Turin: Bocca, 1896).

———, *La criminalità e le vicende economiche d'Italia* (Turin, 1894).

Foscolo, Ugo, *Ultime lettere di Jacopo Ortis* (Milan, 1802; repr., Milan: Mondadori, 1986).

Fratini, Gianmaria, *La patogenesi del suicidio* (Udine, 1910).

Gelli, Jacopo, *Corte d'onore permanente in Firenze* (Florence: de Angelis, 1888).

———, *Duelli celebri* (Milan: Hoepli, 1928).

———, *Duelli mortali del secolo XIX* (Milan: Batistelli, 1899).

———, *Il duello nella storia della giurisprudenza e nella pratica italiana* (Florence: Loescher, 1886).

———, *Manuale del duellante* (Milan, 1896).

Goethe, Johann von, *Die Leiden des Jungen Werthers* (*The Sorrows of Young Werther*),1774.

Gramsci, Antonio, *Prison Notebooks* (New York: International Publishers, 1971).

Guerrieri, R., and Ettore Fornasari di Verce, *I Sensi e le anomalie somatiche nella donna normale e nella prostituta* (Turin: Bocca, 1893).

Hawthorne, Nathaniel, *The Marble Faun* (1860).

Hume, David, "Essay on Suicide" (1777).

Huysmans, J.K. *À rebours* (Paris, 1884; *Against Nature*, New York: Penguin, 1959).

Krafft-Ebbing, Richard, *Psychopathia Sexualis* (Berlin, 1882).

Leggiardi-Laura, C., *Il Delinquente nei 'Promessi Sposi'* (Turin: Bocca, 1899).

Lessona, Carlo, *Il duello nei nuovi studi e nelle nuove idee* (Pisa: editore Spoerri, 1901).

Liberatore, Matteo, *Del diritto sulla vita per quel che concerne il suicidio, il duello, la pena di morte* (Naples, 1845).

Lombroso, Cesare, and Ferrero, Gina Lombroso, *La donna delinquente, la prostituta, e la donna normale* (Turin: Bocca, 1893/1915).

Lombroso, Cesare, *Crime: Its Causes and Remedies* (London: Heinemann, 1911).

———, *Genio e degenerazione* (Palermo: Remo Sandron, 1897).

———, *L'uomo delinquente* (Milan: Hoepli, 1876).

———, *L'uomo di genio* (Turin: Bocca, 1894).

Lovati, C., *Il duello: conversazioni di un avvocato* (Milan, 1908).

Manzoni, Alessandro, *I promessi sposi* (1827).

Machiavelli, Niccolò, *The Prince*, and *Discourses* (1513-14).

Marinetti, F.T., ed. Flint, R.W., *Let's Murder the Moonshine: Selected Writings of F.T. Marinetti* (Los Angeles: Sun & Moon Press, 1991).

————, *La cucina futurista: Futurist Cookbook* (San Francisco: Bedford Arts, 1989).

————, and Corra, Bruno, *L'Isola dei Baci: Romanzo erotico-sociale* (Milan: Studio editoriale lombardo, 1918).

Massarotti, Vito, *Il suicidio nella vita e nella società moderna* (Rome, 1913).

Mazzini, Giuseppe, *Selected Writings,* ed. N. Gangulee (London: Lindsay Drummond, 1945).

Modugno, Nicola, *Il duello* (Bari, 1880).

————, *Pena capitale e duello* (Naples, 1869).

Molinini, Niccolo, *Il suicidio e il duello nella concezione fascista* (Bari, 1934).

Mondello-Nestler, Andrea, *Il suicidio come delitto antinaturale ed anticristiano considerato nella sua origine e nei spaventevoli progressi* (Rome, 1877).

Montaigne, *Essays* (1595).

Morasso, Mario, *Domus Aurea: La reggia, la festa, l'amore a Venezia* (Turin: Bocca, 1908).

————, *Il Nuovo aspetto meccanico del mondo* (Milan: Hoepli, 1907).

————, *La nuova guerra: armi, combattimenti, battaglie* (Milan: Treves, 1914).

————, *La vita moderna nell'arte* (Turin: Bocca, 1904).

————, *Uomini e idee del domani: L'egoarchia* (Turin: Bocca, 1898).

More, Thomas, *Utopia* (1516).

Morello, V., *L'Amore Emigra* (Rome: Tipografia editrice nazionale, 1912).

Morselli, Enrico, *Il Suicidio: Saggio di statistica morale comparata* (Milan: Dumolard, 1879).

————, *Le leggi statistiche del suicidio* (Milan: Civella, 1885).

————, *Suicide: An Essay on Comparative Moral Statistics* (New York: Appleton, 1903).

Motta, Emilio, *Bibliografia del suicidio* (Bellinzona: Salvioni, 1890).

Nicoletti, Jacopo, *Del duello civile e militare ed argomenti atti a distruggerlo* (Florence: Tipografia nazionale, 1904).

Nordau, Max, *Degeneration* (Berlin, 1892).

Nunes, Alberto Franco, *Del duello e dei mezzi più opportuni a bandirlo dalla società* (Turin: Unione tipografia editrice, 1865).

Ojetti, Ugo, *Il monumento a Vittorio Emanuele in Roma e le sue avventure* (Milan: Treves, 1907).

Ottolenghi, S., and Rossi V., *Duecento criminali e prostitute: studiate nei laboratori di clinica psichiatrica e di antropologia di Torino* (Turin: Bocca, 1898).

Palazzeschi, Aldo, *I poeti futuristi* (Milan, 1912).

Papini, Giovanni, *L'uomo finito* (Florence: Vallecchi, 1913).

————, *Maschilità* (Florence: Vallecchi, 1915).

Patrizi, M.L., *La fisiologia d'un bandito: Musolino* (Turin: Bocca, 1904).

————, *Saggio psico-antropologico su Giacomo Leopardi e la sua famiglia* (Turin: Bocca, 1896).

Pesci, Ugo, *I primi anni di Roma capitale* (Rome, 1907).

Proal, Louis, *Le crime et les suicides passionnels* (Paris: Alcan, 1900).

————, *L'education et le suicide des enfants* (Paris: Alcan, 1907).

Rajna, Pio, *Le corti d'amore* (Milan: Hoepli, 1890).

Ravizza, Carlo, *Il suicidio, il sacrificio della vita e il duello* (Milan: Branca 1843).

Ricchini, Luigi, *Tentati suicidi e suicidi con particolare riguardo alla città di Venezia* (Venice, 1903).

Rowbotham, J.F., *The Troubadours and Courts of Love* (London: Swan Sonnschein, 1895).

Russo-Ajello, Antonio, *Il duello secondo i principii, la dottrina, la legislazione* (Città di Castello, 1906).

Sabatini, Concettino, *Dello attentato all propria vita* (Catanzaro: Calabro, 1902).

Serra, Renato, ed. Isnenghi, Mario, *Scritti letterari, morali e politici: saggi e articoli dal 1900 al 1915* (Turin: Einaudi, 1974).

Sighele, Scipio, *La coppia criminale: studio di psicologia morbosa* (Turin: Bocca, 1892).

————, *Letteratura tragica* (Milan, Treves, 1906).

Sorel, Georges, *Reflexions sur la violence* (Paris, 1906; New York: Free Press, 1950).

————, *Les Illusions du progres* (Paris, 1908; Berkeley: University of California Press, 1969).

Symonds, John Addington, *The Letters of John Addington Symonds*, Herbert M. Schueller and Robert L. Peters, eds., (Detroit: Wayne State University Press, 1967).

Tagliabue, Antonio, *Il duello* (Milan, 1867).

————, *Il suicidio* (Milan: Croci, 1871).

Tamassia, Arrigo, *Sull'inversione dell'istinto sessuale* (Reggio Emilia, 1878).

Truffi, Riccardo, *Giostre e cantori di giostre* (Rocca San Casciano, Cappelli, 1911).

Verga, Giovanni, *Novelle rusticane* (Milan, 1883).

Villani, Ferdinando, *Il suicidio innanzi alla ragione e del diritto per l'avvocato* (Trani, 1866).

Voltaire, *Du Suicide* (1764).

Zuccoli, Luciano, *I lussuriosi* (Milan: Barion, 1925).

Zuppetta, Luigi, *Del suicidio in rapporto alla morale ed al diritto* (Naples: Anfossi, 1885).

Zweig, Stefan, *The World of Yesterday* (New York: Viking, 1943; Lincoln: University of Nebraska Press, 1964).

Articles

Loos, Adolf, "Ornament and Crime," (Vienna, 1908) in Ulrich Conrads, ed., *Programs and Manifestoes on 20th-Century Architecture* (Cambridge: MIT Press, 1975), pp. 19–24.

Riegl, Alois, "The Modern Cult of Monuments: Its Character and Its Origin," (Berlin, 1903) in Kurt W. Forster, ed., *Monument/Memory, Oppositions*, Fall 1982, no. 25 (New York: Institute for Architecture and Urban Studies/Rizzoli), pp. 21–51.

Simmel, Georg, "The Metropolis and Mental Life," (Berlin, 1903) in Donald Levine, ed., *On Individuality and Social Forms* (Chicago: University of Chicago Press, 1971), pp. 324–39.

Secondary sources

Books

Adamson, Walter, *Avant-garde Florence: From Modernism to Fascism* (Cambridge: Harvard University Press, 1993).

Agocs, Sandor, *The Troubled Origins of the Italian Catholic Labor Movement* (Detroit: Wayne State University Press, 1988).

Alatri, Paolo, *L'Italia di Giolitti* (Milan: Teti, 1981).

Aldrich, Robert, *The Seduction of the Mediterranean: Writing, Art and Homosexual Fantasy* (London: Routledge, 1993).

Alvarez, A., *The Savage God: A Study of Suicide* (New York: Random House, 1970).

Amfitheatrof, Erik, *The Enchanted Ground: Americans in Italy, 1760-1980* (Boston: Little, Brown and Company, 1980).

Anderson, Olive, *Suicide in Victorian and Edwardian England* (New York: Oxford University Press, 1987).

Anglo, Sydney, *Chivalry in the Renaissance* (Woodbridge, UK: Boydell Press, 1990).

Angri, Gin, *Como: guida alla storia, all'arte, all'attualità* (Como: New Press, 1981)

Aries, Philippe, *Western Attitudes toward Death from the Middle Ages to the Present* (Baltimore: Johns Hopkins University Press, 1974).

Bagatti, Fabrizio, ed., *Futurismo a Firenze: 1910–1920* (Florence: Sansoni, 1984).

Victor Bailey, *This Rash Act: Suicide Across the Life Cycle in the Victorian City* (Stanford: Stanford University Press, 1998).

Banham, Reyner, *Theory and Design in the First Machine Age* (Cambridge: Cambridge University Press, 1960).

Barber, Richard, *The Knight and Chivalry* (New York: Harper & Row, 1982).

Barron, Stephanie, editor/curator, *Degenerate Art: The Fate of the Avant-garde in Nazi Germany* (Los Angeles: LACMA, 1991).

Belli, Gabriela, and Rella, Franco, *Divisionismo Italiano* (Milan: Electa, 1990).

Belli, Gabriela, and Rella, Franco, *L'età del Divisionismo* (Milan: Electa, 1990).

Benjamin, Walter, *Illuminations* (New York: Schocken, 1969).

Benko, Stephen, *Pagan Rome and the Early Christians* (Bloomington: Indiana University Press, 1986).

Bercovitch, Sacvan, *The Puritan Origins of the American Self* (New Haven: Yale University Press, 1975).

Bernardini, Aldo, *Cinema muto italiano: Arte, divismo e mercato* (Rome: Laterza, 1981).

Biasin, Gian Paolo, *Literary Diseases: Theme and Metaphor in the Italian Novel* (Austin: University of Texas Press, 1975).

Billacois, Francois, *The Duel: Its Rise and Fall in Early Modern France* (New Haven: Yale University Press, 1990).

Billington, James H., *The Icon and the Axe: An Interpretive History of Russian Culture* (New York: Vintage, 1970).

Black, Christopher, *Italian Confraternities in the Sixteenth Century* (New York: Cambridge University Press, 1989).

Blackbourn, David, and Eley, Geoff, *The Peculiarities of German History* (New York: Oxford University Press, 1984).

Blackbourn, David, and Evans, Richard, *The German Bourgeoisie: Essays on the social history of the German middle class from the late eighteenth to the early twentieth century* (London: Routledge, 1991).

Blum, Carol, *Rousseau and the Republic of Virtue: The Language of Politics in the French Revolution* (Ithaca: Cornell University Press, 1986).

Bohstedt, John, *Riots and Community Politics in England and Wales, 1790–1810* (Cambridge: Harvard University Press, 1983).

———, *Riots as Popular Politics in the Modern West* (London: McMillan 1992).

Bondanella, Peter, *The Eternal City: Roman Images in the Modern World* (Chapel Hill: University of North Carolina Press, 1987).

Bortolotti, Franca Pieroni, *Alle origini del movimento femminile in Italia: 1848–1892* (Turin: Einaudi, 1963).

Bosworth, Richard, *Italy, the Least of the Great Powers* (Cambridge: Cambridge University Press, 1979).

————, *Italy and the Approach of the First World War* (London: MacMillan, 1983).

————, and Romano, Sergio, eds., *La politica estera italiana, 1860–1985* (Bologna: Il Mulino, 1991).

Bremmer, Jan, and Roodenburg, Herman, *A Cultural History of Gesture* (Ithaca: Cornell University Press, 1991).

Brenni, Luigi, *La tessitura serica attraverso i secoli: Cenni sulle sue origini e il suo sviluppo in Como, nelle altre città italiane ed in alcuni stati europei* (Como: Ostinelli, 1925).

Brentano, Robert, *Rome Before Avignon: A Social History of Thirteenth Century Rome* (Berkeley: University of California Press, 1991).

Broggi, Tito, *Storia del setificio comasco, vol. II* (Como: Centro Lariano, 1967).

Brown, Norman O., *Life Against Death: The Psychoanalytic Meaning of History* (Middletown: Wesleyan University Press, 1959).

Brown, Peter, *The Body and Society: Men, Women, and Sexual Renunciation in Early Christianity* (New York: Columbia University Press, 1988).

Buck-Morss, Susan, *The Dialectics of Seeing: Walter Benjamin and the Arcades Project* (Cambridge, MA: MIT Press, 1989).

Bulferetti, Luigi, *Cesare Lombroso* (Turin: Unione tipografico editrice torinese, 1975).

Burke, Peter, *The Historical Anthropology of Early Modern Italy: Essays on Perception and Communication* (Cambridge: Cambridge University Press, 1987).

———, *Popular Culture in Early Modern Europe* (New York: Harper & Row, 1978).

———, *The Historical Anthropology of Early Modern Italy: Essays on Perception and Communication* (Cambridge: Cambridge University Press, 1987).

———, and Porter, Roy, *The Social History of Language* (Cambridge: Cambridge University Press, 1987).

Burkert, Walter, Girard, Rene, and Smith, Jonathan Z., *Violent Origins: Ritual Killing and Cultural Formation* (Stanford: Stanford University Press, 1987).

Cafagna, Luciano, *Il nord nella storia d'Italia* (Bari: Laterza, 1962).

Caizzi, Bruno, *Storia del setificio comasco, vol. I* (Como: Centro Lariano, 1957).

Cambon, Glauco, *Ugo Foscolo: Poet of Exile* (Princeton: Princeton University Press, 1981).

Candeloro, Giorgio, *Storia dell'Italia moderna* (Milan: Feltrinelli, vol. VI, 1970; vol. VII, 1974; repr. 1986).

Canetti, Elias, *Crowds and Power* (New York: Farrar, Straus, Giroux, 1984; orig. *Masse und Macht*, (Hamburg: Claassen, 1960).

Caracciolo, Alberto, *Roma capitale, dal risorgimento alla crisi dello stato liberale* (Rome: Rinascita, 1956).

Carpanetto, Dino, and Ricuperati, Giuseppe, *Italy in the Age of Reason, 1685-1789* (London: Longman, 1987).

Cesarini, Paolo, *Tutti gli anni di Tozzi* (Montepulciano: del Grifo, 1982).

Chabod, F, *Storia della politica estera italiana dal 1870 al 1896* (Bari: Laterza, 1965).

Cherniavsky, Michael, *Tsar and People: Studies in Russian Myths* (New York: Random House, 1969).

Chiti, Luigi, *Cultura e politica nelle riviste fiorentine nel primo novecento, 1903-1915* (Turin: Loescher, 1972).

Cipolla, Carlo, *Faith, Reason, and the Plague in Seventeenth-Century Tuscany*, trans. Muriel Kittel (New York: Norton, 1981; orig. Bologna: Il Mulino, 1977).

Cohn, Norman, *The Pursuit of the Millennium: Revolutionary Millenarians and Mystical Anarchists of the Middle Ages* (New York: Oxford University Press, 1961).

Colapietra, Raffaele, *Storia del parlamento italiano* (Palermo: Flaccovio, 1976).
Colombo, Giorgo, *La scienza infelice: il museo di antropologia criminale di Cesare Lombroso* (Turin: Boringhieri, 1975).

Cooper, Sandi, *Patriotic Pacifism: The political vision of Italian peace movements, 1867–1915* (Los Angeles: California State University Occasional Papers, 1985).

————, *Patriotic Pacifism: Waging War on War in Europe, 1815–1914* (New York: Oxford University Press, 1991).

Crary, Jonathan, *Techniques of the Observer: On Vision and Modernity in the Nineteenth Century* (Cambridge, MA: MIT Press, 1990).

Crepet, Paolo, and Francesco Florenzano, eds., *Il Rifiuto di vivere: anatomia del suicidio* (Rome: Editori Riuniti, 1989).

Crispolti, Enrico, *Storia e critica del Futurismo* (Rome: Laterza, 1987).

Critelli, Claudio, and Pigni, Elio, *L'artigianato, i servizi, la città: Esperienze di lavoro artigianale in Como tra il 1400 e il 1911* (Como: Archivio di Stato, 1988).

Crompton, Louis, *Byron and Greek Love* (Berkeley: University of California Press, 1985).

Cross, Tim, *The Lost Voices of World War I* (Iowa City: University of Iowa Press, 1989).

D'Agostino, Francesco, ed., *Diritto e corporeità: prospettive filosofiche e profili giuridici della disponabilità del corpo umano* (Milan: Jaca Book, 1984).

Darnton, Robert, *The Great Cat Massacre and Other Episodes in French Cultural History* (New York: Vintage, 1985).

Davis, John A., *Conflict and Control: Law and Order in Nineteenth-Century Italy* (Atlantic Highlands, NJ: Humanities Press International, 1988).

———, and Ginsbourg, Paul, eds., *Society and Politics in the Age of the Risorgimento* (Cambridge: Cambridge University Press, 1991).

Davis, Natalie Zemon, *Society and Culture in Early Modern France* (Stanford: Stanford University Press, 1975).

De Feo, Italo, *Leopardi: l'uomo e l'opera* (Milan: Mondadori, 1972).

De Grand, Alexander, *Italian Fascism: Its Origins and Development* (Lincoln: University of Nebraska Press, 1982).

———, *The Italian Nationalist Association and the Rise of Fascism in Italy* (Lincoln: University of Nebraska Press, 1978).

De Grazia, Victoria, *How Fascism Ruled Women: Italy, 1922–1945* (Berkeley: University of California Press, 1992).

———, *The Culture of Consent: Mass Organization of Leisure in Fascist Italy* (Cambridge: Cambridge University Press, 1981).

De Maddalena, Aldo, *Centocinquant'anni di vita economica mantovana, 1815–1965* (Mantua: Camera di Commercio, 1967).

De Maria, Luciano, *La nascita dell'avanguardia: Saggi sul futurismo italiano* (Venice: Marsilio, 1986).

De Micheli, *Le avanguardie artistiche del novecento* (Milan: Feltrinelli, 1986).

Dell'Arco, Mario, *Pasquino: Statua parlante* (Rome: Bulzoni, 1967).

Della Peruta, Franco, *Milano, lavoro e fabbrica: 1884-1915* (Milan: F. Angeli, 1987).

Dijkstra, Bram, *Idols of Perversity: Fantasies of Feminine Evil in Fin-de-Siècle Culture* (New York: Oxford University Press, 1986).

Dolino, Gianni, *Orgoglio e pregiudizio: L'Eros lesbico e omosessuale nella letteratura del Novecento* (Turin, 1983).

Drake, Richard, *Byzantium for Rome: The Politics of Nostalgia in Umbertian Italy, 1878–1900* (Chapel Hill: University of North Carolina Press, 1980).

Droge, Arthur, and Tabor James D., *A Noble Death: Suicide and Martyrdom Among Christians and Jews in Antiquity* (San Francisco: Harper Collins, 1992).

Duby, Georges, *The Chivalrous Society* (Berkeley: University of California Press, 1980).

Eco, Umberto, *The Limits of Interpretation* (Bloomington: Indiana University Press, 1994).

Editori del Villaggio, *Bachicoltura e la confezione del seme bachi in Italia* (Milan: Lanzani, 1909).

Eksteins, Modris, *Rites of Spring: The Great War and the Birth of the Modern Age* (New York: Doubleday, 1990).

Evans, E.P., *The Criminal Prosecution and Capital Punishment of Animals: The Lost History of Europe's Animal Trials* (1906), (London: Faber and Faber, 1987).

Evans, Richard, *In Hitler's Shadow: West German Historians and the Attempt to Escape from the Nazi Past* (New York: Pantheon, 1989).

———, *Rethinking German History: Nineteenth Century Germany and the Origins of the Third Reich* (New York: Unwin Hyman, 1987).

———, *Lying About Hitler* (New York: Basic Books, 2001).

Falqui, Enrico, *Indice della Voce e di Lacerba* (Florence, Vallchi, 1966).

———, *Tutte le poesie della Voce* (Florence: Vallecchi, 1966).

Fedden, Henry Romilly, *Suicide: A Social and Historical Study* (London: Peter Davies, Ltd., 1938).

Fedele, Santi, and Restifo, Giuseppe, *Il fascismo: politica e vita sociale* (Milan: Teti, 1980).

Ferrone, Siro, ed., *Teatro dell'Italia unita* (Milan: il Saggiatore, 1980).

Frevert, Ute, *Satisfaktion! Das Duell in der burgerlichen Gesellschaft* (Munich, 1991).

Frigessi, Delia Castelnuovo, *La cultura italiana del '900 attraverso le riviste* (Turin: Einaudi, 1970).

Furet, Francois, *Penser la Revolution francaise* (Paris: Gallimard, 1978).

Fussell, Paul, *The Great War and Modern Memory* (Oxford: Oxford University Press, 1975).

Gabrieli, Manlio, *La prima amministrazione provinciale socialista in Italia: Mantova, 1904–1905* (Mantua: Casa della Mantegna, 1986).

Gentile, Emilio, *Il mito dello stato nuovo dall'antigiolittismo al fascismo* (Rome: Laterza, 1982).

————, *L'Italia giolittiana: la storia e la critica* (Rome: Laterza, 1977).

Gerschenkron, Alexander, *Economic Backwardness in Historical Perspective* (Cambridge: Cambridge University Press, 1962).

Gherarducci, Isabella, *Il futurismo italiano: materiali e testimonianze critiche* (Rome: Editori Riuniti, 1976).

Ghirelli, Antonio, *Storia del calcio in Italia* (Turin: Einaudi, 1954).

Ghisalberti, Carlo, *La codificazione del diritto in Italia, 1865-1942* (Rome: Laterza, 1985).

Gies, Frances, *The Knight in History* (New York: Harper & Row, 1984).

Gilman, Sander, *Disease and Representation: Images of Illness from Madness to AIDS* (Ithaca: Cornell University Press, 1988).

Gould, Stephen Jay, *Ontogeny and Phylogeny* (Cambridge: Belknap Press, 1977).

Greenberg, David F., *The Construction of Homosexuality* (Chicago: University of Chicago Press, 1988).

Grey, Ian, *Ivan III and the Unification of Russia* (New York: Collier, 1967).

Guernsey, R.S., *Suicide: history of the penal laws relating to it in their legal, social, moral, and religious aspects, in ancient and modern times* (New York: L.K. Strouse & Co., 1883).

Gurevich, Aron, *Medieval Popular Culture: Problems of Belief and Perception* (Cambridge: Cambridge University Press, 1988).

Hales, E.E.Y., *Pio Nono: A Study in European Politics and Religion in the Nineteenth Century* (Garden City: Doubleday, 1962).

Hamilton, Edith, *Mythology* (New York: Mentor, 1963).

Harrison, Thomas, *1910: The Emancipation of Desire* (Berkeley: University of California Press, 1996).

Herf, Jeffrey, *Reactionary Modernism: Technology, Culture and Politics in Weimar and the Third Reich* (Cambridge: Cambridge University Press, 1981).

Hobbes, Thomas, *Leviathan* (London, 1651).

Hobsbawm, Eric, *Bandits* (New York: Pantheon, 1981).

————, *Nations and Nationalism Since 1780: Programme, Myth, Reality* (Cambridge: Cambridge University Press, 1990).

————, *Primitive Rebels: Studies in Archaic Forms of Social Movement in the 19th and 20th Centuries* (New York: Norton, 1965).

————, and Ranger, Terrence, eds., *The Invention of Tradition* (Cambridge: Cambridge University Press, 1983).

Huizinga, Johann, *Homo Ludens: A Study of the Play Element in Culture* (1938; Boston: Beacon Press, 1955).

Hulten, Pontius, *Futurism and Futurisms* (New York: Abbeville Press, 1989).

Hunt, Lynn, *Politics, Culture, and Class in the French Revolution* (Berkeley: University of California Press, 1984).

Isnenghi, Mario, *Il mito della grande guerra* (Bologna: Il Mulino, 1989).

————, *Le guerre degli italiani: Parole, immagini, ricordi, 1848–1945* (Milan: Mondadori, 1989).

Istituto per la storia del Risorgimento italiano, *Roma nell'età giolittiana: L'amministrazione Nathan* (Rome: edizioni dell'Ateneo, 1984).

Jaccobi, Ruggero, *Poesia futurista italiana* (Parma, 1968).

Joll, James, *Three Intellectuals in Politics: Blum, Rathenau, Marinetti* (New York: Pantheon, 1960).

Jones, Gareth Stedman, *Languages of Class: Studies in English Working Class History, 1832–1982* (Cambridge: Cambridge University Press, 1983).

Kern, Stephen, *The Culture of Time and Space, 1880–1918* (Cambridge: Harvard University Press, 1983).

Kertzer, David I., *Sacrificed for Honor: Italian Infant Abandonment and the Politics of Reproductive Control* (Boston: Beacon Press, 1993).

———, *The Kidnapping of Edgardo Mortara* (New York: Knopf, 1997).

Kiernan, V.G., *The Duel in European History: Honour and the Reign of Aristocracy* (Oxford: Oxford University Press, 1988).

Kirby, Michael and Victoria Nes, *Futurist Performance* (New York: PAJ, 1986).

Klaits, Joseph, *Servants of Satan: The Age of the Witch Hunts* (Bloomington: Indiana University Press, 1985).

Kobak, Annette, *Isabelle: The Life of Isabelle Eberhardt* (New York: Vintage, 1990).

Koon, Tracy, *Believe, Obey, Fight: Political Socialization of Youth in Fascist Italy, 1922–1943* (Chapel Hill: University of North Carolina Press, 1985).

Koshar, Rudy, ed., *Splintered Classes: Politics and the Lower Middle Classes in Interwar Europe* (New York: Holmes & Maier, 1990).

Kostoff, Spiro, *A History of Architecture: Settings and Rituals* (New York: Oxford University Press, 1985).

———, *The Third Rome: Traffic and Glory* (Berkeley: University of California Press, 1973).

Ladurie, Emmanuel LeRoy, *Le Carnaval de Romans* (Paris: Gallimard, 1979).

Laqueur, Thomas, *Making Sex: Body and Gender from the Greeks to Freud* (Cambridge: Harvard University Press, 1990).

Levi, Alessandro, *Ricordi della vita e dei tempi di Ernesto Nathan* (Florence: LeMonnier, 1954).

Large, David C., and Weber, William, eds., *Wagnerism in European Culture and Politics* (Itahca: Cornell University Press, 1984).

Lill, Rudolf, and Valsecchi, Franco, eds., *Il nazionalismo in Italia e in Germania fino alla prima guerra mondiale* (Bologna: Mulino, 1981).

Lincoln, Bruce, *Death, War, and Sacrifice: Studies in Ideology and Practice* (Chicago: University of Chicago Press, 1991).

Lista, Giovanni, *Arte e politica: Il futurismo di sinistra in Italia* (Milan: Multhipla, 1980).

Lombroso, Gina, *Cesare Lombroso: storia della vita e delle opere* (Bologna: Zanichelli, 1921).

Lowe, Donald M., *History of Bourgeois Perception* (Chicago: University of Chicago Press, 1982).

Lyttleton, Adrian, ed., *Italian Fascisms: From Pareto to Gentile* (New York: Harper & Row, 1973).

Macioti, Maria I., *Ernesto Nathan: un sindaco che non ha fatto scuola* (Rome: Editrice Iuana, 1983).

Mack Smith, Denis, *The Making of Modern Italy, 1796–1870* (New York: Harper & Row, 1968).

———, *Italy and Its Monarchy* (New Haven: Yale University Press, 1989).

———, *Italy* (Ann Arbor: University of Michigan, 1959).

Maier, Charles S., *Recasting Bourgeois Europe: Stabilization in France, Germany, and Italy in the Decade after World War I* (Princeton: Princeton University Press, 1975).

Mandell, Richard D., *Sport: A Cultural History* (New York: Columbia University Press, 1984).

Mannheim, Hermann, *Pioneers in Criminology* (Chicago: Quadrangle, 1960).

Martin, John Rupert, *Baroque* (New York: Harper & Row, 1977).

Martin, Marianne W., *Futurist Art and Theory* (New York: Hacker, 1978).

Martines, Lauro, *Violence and Civil Disorder in Italian Cities: 1200-1500* (Berkeley, University of California Press, 1972).

Marx, Karl, *The 18th Brumaire of Louis Bonaparte* (1852; New York: International Publishers, 1963).

Mayer, Arno, *The Persistence of the Old Regime: Europe to the Great War* (New York: Pantheon, 1981).

McAleer, Kevin, *Dueling: The Cult of Honor in Fin-de-Siècle Germany* (Princeton: Princeton University Press, 1994).

McGann, Jerome J., *The Beauty of Inflections: Literary Investigations in Historical Method and Theory* (New York: Oxford University Press, 1985).

Merli, Stefano, *Proletariato di fabbrica e capitalismo industriale: il caso italiano, 1880–1890* (Florence: La Nuova Italia, 1972).

Minois, Georges, (Lydia G. Cochrane, trans.), *History of Suicide: Voluntary Death in Western Culture* (Baltimore: Johns Hopkins University Press, 1999). Orig. pub. *Histoire du suicide: La societè occidentale face à la mort volontaire* (Paris: Libraire Artheme Fayard, 1995).

Mitchell, B.R., *European Historical Statistics, 1750–1970* (London: McMillan, 1978).

Mitchell, Timothy, *Blood Sport: A Social History of Spanish Bullfighting* (Philadelphia: University of Pennsylvania Press, 1991).

Mola, Aldo, *Istituzioni e metodi politici dell'età giolittiana* (Turin: Centro studi piemontesi, 1979).

Mori, Giorgio, *L'industrializazzione in Italia, 1861–1900* (Bologna: Il Mulino, 1977).

Morselli, Guido, *Divertimento 1889* (Milan: Adelphi, 1975).

Mosse, George, *Confronting the Nation: Jewish and Western Nationalism* (Hanover: University Press of New England, 1993).

———, *Fallen Soldiers: Reshaping the Memory of the World Wars* (New York: Oxford University Press, 1990).

———, *Masses and Man: Nationalist and Fascist Perceptions of Reality* (Detroit: Wayne State University Press, 1987).

———, *Nationalism and Sexuality: Middle Class Morality and Sexual Norms in Modern Europe* (Madison: University of Wisconsin Press, 1985).

———, *The Nationalization of the Masses: Political Symbolism and Mass Movements in Germany from the Napoleonic Wars through the Third Reich* (Ithaca: Cornell University Press, 1975).

———, *Toward the Final Solution: A History of European Racism* (Madison: University of Wisconsin Press, 1978).

Muir, Edward, *Sex and Gender in Historical Perspective* (Baltimore: Johns Hopkins University Press, 1990).

———, and Ruggiero, Guido, eds., *Microhistory and the Lost Peoples of Europe* (Baltimore: Johns Hopkins University Press, 1991).

Nascimbene, *Il movimento operaio in Italia: La questione sociale a Milano dal 1890 al 1900* (Milan: Cisalpino-Goliardica, 1972).

Neubauer, John, *The Fin-de-Siècle Culture of Adolescence* (New Haven: Yale University Press, 1992).

Nolthenius, Helene, *Duecento: The Late Middle Ages in Italy* (New York: McGraw-Hill, 1968).

Novak, David, *Suicide and morality: the theories of Plato, Aquinas, and Kant and their relevance for suicidology* (New York: Scholars Studies Press, 1975).

Nozzoli, Anna and Simonetti, Carlo Maria, *Il tempo de 'La Voce'* (Florence: Vallecchi, 1982).

Nye, Robert, *Crime, Madness, & Politics in Modern France: The Medical Concept of National Decline* (Princeton: Princeton University Press, 1984).

————, *Masculinity and Male Codes of Honor in Modern France* (New York: Oxford University Press, 1993).

Omodeo, Adolfo, *Momenti della vita di guerra: Dai diari e dalle lettere dei caduti, 1915–1918* (1935; Turin: Einaudi, 1968).

Oosterhuis, Harry, and Kennedy, Hubert, *Homosexuality and Male Bonding in pre-Nazi Germany* (New York: Haworth Press, 1991).

Origo, Iris, *Leopardi: A Study in Solitude* (London: Hamish Hamilton, 1953).

Orrigoni, Carlo, *Il suicidio in Foscolo* (Turin: Einaudi, 1951).

Oselini, Gabriele, *La situazione socio-economica del mantovano alla vigilia della prima guerra mondiale* (Parma: unpublished dissertation, 1975).

Ozouf, Mona, *La Fête revolutionnaire, 1789-1799* (Paris: Gallimard, 1976).

Paliotti, Vittorio, *Il Salone Margherita e la belle epoque: Napoli tra fine Ottocento e primo Novecento* (Rome: Benincasa, 1975).

Palmer, Bryan, *Descent into Discourse: The Reification of Language and the Writing of Social History* (Philadelphia: Temple University Press, 1990).

Pancaldi, Giuliano, *Darwin in Italy: Science Across Cultural Frontiers* (Bloomington: Indiana University Press, 1991).

Papa, Emilio, *Fascismo e cultura* (Venice: Marsilia, 1974).

Partner, Peter, *Renaissance Rome, 1500–1559: A Portrait of a Society* (Berkeley: University of California Press, 1979).

Pasolini, Pier Paolo, *Roman Nights and Other Stories*, trans. John Shepley (Marlboro, VT: Marlboro Press, 1986).

————, *Roman Poems*, trans. Lawrence Ferlinghetti and Francesca Valente (San Francisco: City Lights, 1986).

————, *Poems*, trans. Norman MacAfee and Luciano Martinengo (New York: Vintage, 1982).

Patalano, Vincenzo, *I delitti contro la vita* (Padua: CEDAM, 1984).

Perloff, Marjorie, *The Futurist Moment: Avant-Garde, Avant-Guerre, and the Language of Rupture* (Chicago: University of Chicago Press, 1986).

Piantoni De Angeles, Gianna, *Mitologia e iconografia del XX secolo nel manifesto italiano dal 1895 al 1914* (Rome: De Luca, 1979).

————, *Roma 1911* (Rome: De Luca, 1980).

Pick, Daniel, *Faces of Degeneration: A European Disorder, c. 1848–c. 1918* (Cambridge: Cambridge University Press, 1989).

Pilbeam, Pamela, *The Middle Classes in Europe, 1789–1914* (London: McMillan, 1990).

Plass, Paul, *The Game of Death in Ancient Rome: Arena Sport and Political Suicide* (Madison: University of Wisconsin Press, 1995).

Poggioli, Renato, *The Theory of the Avant-Garde* (1962; Cambridge: Harvard University Press, 1968).

Pounds, Norman, J.G., *An historical geography of Europe, 1800–1914* (Cambridge: Cambridge University Press, 1985).

Pozzolini, Alberto, *Le origini del movimento operaio e contadino in Italia* (Bologna: Zanichelli, 1971).

Pratolini, Vasco, *Metello* (Milan: Mondadori, 1955).

Quetel, Claude, *Le Mal de Naples: histoire de la syphilis* (Paris: Seghers, 1986).

Ramella, Franco, *Terra e telai: sistemi di parentela e manifattura nel Biellese dell'ottocento* (Turin: Einaudi, 1983).

Rebustini, Isabella, *Popolazione e attività economiche di Mantova dall'Unità d'Italia alla vigilia della prima guerra mondiale* (Parma: unpublished dissertation, 1975).

Rendina, Claudio, *Il Vaticano: Storia e segreti; il sacro e il profano in due milenni della Santa Sede* (Rome: Newton Compton, 1986).

Robertson, Priscilla, *Revolutions of 1848: A Social History* (New York: Harper & Row, 1960).

Rofes, Eric, *I Thought People Like That Killed Themselves* (San Francisco: Grey Fox Press, 1983).

Rolfs, Daniel, *The Last Cross: A History of Suicide in Italian Literature* (Ravenna: Longo, 1981).

Rocke, Michael, *Forbidden Friendships: Homosexuality and Male Culture in Renaissance Florence* (New York: Oxford University Press, 1996).

Sabine, Lorenzo, *Notes on Duels and Duelling* (Boston: Crosby, Nichols & Co., 1855).

Said, Edward, *Orientalism* (New York: Vintage, 1979).

Salinari, Carlo, *Miti e coscienza del decadentismo italiano: D'Annunzio, Pascoli, Fogazzaro, e Pirandello* (Milan: Feltrinelli, 1960).

Sanguinetti, Edoardo, *Ideologia e linguaggio* (Milan: Feltrinelli, 1970).

Saslow, James M., *Ganymede in the Renaissance: Homosexuality in Art and Society* (New Haven: Yale University Press, 1986).

Scaramucci, Ines, *Le avanguardie del primo novecento: il futurismo* (Milan: CELUC, 1972).

Scrivano, Riccardo, *Il decadentismo e la critica: storia a antologia della critica* (Florence: La Nuova Italia, 1963).

Sedgwick, Eve Kosofsky, *The Epistemology of the Closet* (Berkeley: University of California Press, 1990).

Settembrini, Domenico, *Storia dell'idea antiborghese in Italia, 1860–1989* (Rome: Laterza, 1991).

Severin, Dante, *Figure e momenti di storia comasca* (Como: Camera di Commercio, 1965).

————, *Il problema industriale a Como dopo l'Unità, 1860–1900* (Como: Camera di Commercio, 1983).

————, *La Camera di Commercio a Como e la promozione dell'economia serica, 1860–1900* (Como: Camera di Commercio, 1983).

————, *Lotta politica a Como: Formazione, svolgimento e crisi dei partiti, 1859–1925* (Como: Cairoli, 1975).

————, *Uomini e realtà a Como nel 1859–1915* (Como: La Provincia, 1979).

Simoncini, Giorgio, *Le capitali italiane dal rinascimento al'unità* (Milan: CLUP, 1985).

Skocpol, Theda, *State and Social Revolutions: A Comparative Analysis of France, Russia, and China* (Cambridge: Cambridge University Press, 1979).

Somogyi, Stefano, *Il suicidio in Italia, 1864–1965* (Rome: Tip. Olimpica, 1967).

Sontag, Susan, *Illness as Metaphor* (New York: Vintage, 1978).

Spackman, Barbara, *Decadent Geneaologies: The Rhetoric of Sickness from Baudelaire to d'Annunzio* (Ithaca: Cornell University Press, 1989).

Sparti, Pepa, *L'Italia che cambia: attraverso i manifesti della raccolta Salce* (Florence: Artificio, 1989).

Spirito, Ugo, *Storia del diritto penale italiano: Da Cesare Beccaria ai nostri giorni* (Rome, 1924; Florence: Sansoni, 1974).

Sprigge, Sylvia, *Croce, the King, and the Allies* (London: Allen & Unwin, 1950).

Stille, Alexander, *Benevolence and Betrayal: Five Jewish Families Under Fascism* (New York: Summit Books, 1992).

Sylla, Richard, and Toniolo, Gianni, *Patterns of European Industrialization: The Nineteenth Century* (London: Routledge, 1991).

Tannenbaum, Edward, *The Fascist Experience: Italian Society and Culture, 1922–1945* (New York: Basic Books, 1972).

Tessari, Roberto, *Il mito della macchina: letteratura e industria nel primo novecento italiano* (Milan: Mursia, 1973).

Thea, Paolo, ed., *Nuove tendenze: Milano e l'altro Futurismo* (Milan: Electa, 1980).

Theweleit, Klaus, *Male Fantasies*, 2 vols., (Minneapolis: University of Minnesota Press; 1987, 1989).

Thompson, E.P., *The Making of the English Working Class* (New York: Random House, 1966).

Timms, Edward, and Collier, Peter, *Visions and Blueprints: Avant-garde culture and radical politics in early twentieth-century Europe* (Manchester: Manchester University Press, 1988).

Tisdall, Caroline, and Bozzolla, Angelo, *Futurism* (New York: Oxford University Press, 1978).
Valeri, Nino, *Dalla 'belle epoque' al fascismo* (Rome: Laterza, 1975).

Van Ginneken, Jaap, *Crowds, Psychology, and Politics, 1871–1899* (Cambridge: Cambridge University Press, 1992).

Vance, Carole S., *Pleasure and Danger: Exploring Female Sexuality* (Boston: Routledge, 1984).

Vanzetto, Livio, and Brunetta, Ernesto, *Storia di Treviso* (Padua: Il Poligrafo, 1988).

Venè, Gian Franco, *Mille lire al mese: Vita quotidiana della famiglia nell'Italia fascista* (Milan: Mondadori, 1988).

Vigezzi, Brunello, *Da Giolitti a Salandra* (Florence: Vallecchi, 1969).

Vinci, Antonio, *Prefigurazioni del fascismo* (Milan: CELUC, 1974).

Viviani, Alberto, *Giubbe Rosse: Il caffè fiorentino dei futuristi negli anni incendari, 1913–1915* (1933; Florence: Vallecchi, 1983).

Weber, Eugen, *Peasants into Frenchmen: The Modernization of Rural France, 1870-1914* (Stanford: Stanford University Press, 1976).

Weeks, Jeffrey, *Sexuality and Its Discontents: Meanings, Myths, and Modern Sexualities* (London: Routledge & Kegan Paul, 1985).

Wehler, Hans Ulrich, *The German Empire* (New Hampshire: Berg, 1985).

Weissman, Ronald, *Ritual Brotherhood in Renaissance Florence* (New York: Academic Press, 1982).

Welsford, Enid, *The Fool: His Social and Literary History* (New York: Farrar & Reinhart, 1935).

Whittam, John, *The Politics of the Italian Army, 1861–1918* (London: Crom Helm Ltd., 1977).

Williams, Raymond, *The Politics of Modernism: Against the New Conformists* (London: Verso, 1989).

Winslow, Forbes, *The anatomy of suicide* (London: H. Renshaw, 1840).

Wohl, Robert, *The Generation of 1914* (Cambridge: Harvard University Press, 1979).

Woodward, Anthony, *Rome: Time and Eternity* (Images Publishing: Upton-on-Severn, 1995).

Wunderli, Richard, *Peasant Fires: The Drummer of Niklashausen* (Bloomington: Indiana University Press, 1992).

Zaninelli, Sergio, *Da un sistema agricolo a un sistema industriale: Il Comasco dal settecento al novecento* (Como: Camera di Commercio, 1987).

Zuccotti, Susan, *The Italians and the Holocaust: Persecution, Rescue and Survival* (New York: Basic Books, 1987).

Articles/reviews

Adamson, Walter L., "The Language of Opposition in Early Twentieth-Century Italy: Rhetorical Continuities between Pre-war Florentine Avant-gardism and Mussolini's Fascism," *Journal of Modern History*, 64 (March 1992): pp. 22–51.

Berezin, Mabel, "Created Constituencies: The Italian Middle Classes and Fascism," in Koshar (1990): pp. 142–63.

Burke, Peter, "The language of gesture in early modern Italy," in Bremmer and Roodenburg (1991): pp. 71–83.

Canepa, Giacomo, *"La concezione Antropo-criminologica del suicidio,"* in Centro nazionale di prevenzione e difesa sociale, *Suicidio e tentato suicidio in Italia* (Milan: A. Giuffrè, 1967): pp. 305–18.

Castronuovo, Valerio, "The Italian Take-Off: A Critical Re-Examination of the Problem," *Journal of Italian History*, vol. I, no. (Winter, 1978): pp. 492–510.

Cavallo, Sandra, and Cerutti, Simona, "Female Honor and the Social Control of Reproduction in Piedmont between 1600 and 1800," in Muir and Ruggiero (1990): pp. 73–109.

Cohen, Thomas V., "The Lay Liturgy of Affront in Sixteenth-Century Italy," *Journal of Social History* (Summer, 1992): pp. 857–77.

Dall'Orto, Giovanni, *"Le parole per dirlo: Storia di undici termini relativi all'omosessualità,"* in *Sodoma: rivista omosessuale di cultura*, Anno III, no. 3 (Turin, 1986).

Davies, Judy, "The futures market: Marinetti, and the Fascists of Milan," in Timms and Collier (1988): pp. 82–97.

Dickson, Gary, "The flagellants of 1260 and the crusades," *Journal of Medieval History*, 15 (1989): pp. 227–267.

Drees, Clayton J., "Sainthood and suicide: the motives of the martyrs of Cordoba, a.d. 850-859," *Journal of Medieval and Renaissance Studies*, 20:1 (Spring 1990): pp. 59–89.

Eley, Geoff, and Nield, Keith, "Why Does Social History Ignore Politics?", *Social History*, vol. 5, no. 2 (May 1980): pp. 249–71.

Evans, Richard, "The Myth of Germany's Missing Revolution," *New Left Review*, no. 149 (Jan. 1985): pp. 67–94.

Ferrante, Lucia, "Women in the *Casa del Soccorso di San Paolo* in Sixteenth-Century Bologna," in Muir and Ruggiero (1990): pp. 46–72.

Forcella, Enzo, "Roma 1911: *"Quadri di una esposizione,"* in Piantoni de Angelis (1980): pp. 27–38.

Frevert, Ute, "Bourgeois honor: middle-class duellists in Germany from the late eighteenth to the early twentieth century," in Blackbourn and Evans (1991): pp. 255–92.

Genovese, Eugene, and Genovese, Elizabeth Fox, "The Political Crisis of Social History: A Marxian Perspective," *Journal of Social History*, vol. 10, no. 2 (Winter 1976): pp. 205–220.

Gentile, Emilio, review of Settembrini, Domenico, *Storia dell'idea antiborghese in Italia*, in *Storia contemporanea*, vol. 1, XXIII, (Feb. 1992): pp. 144–51.

Ginzburg, Carlo, et al., "Ritual Pillages: A Preface to Research in Progress," in Muir and Ruggiero (1991): pp. 20–41.

Greenberg, Clement, "Avant-Garde and Kitsch," in Greenberg, *Collected Essays and Criticism*, vol. 1, (Chicago: University of Chicago Press, 1988): pp. 5–22.

Koonz, Claudia, "The Fascist Solution to the Woman Problem in Italy and Germany," in Koonz and Bridenthal, eds., *Becoming Visible: Women in European History* (Boston: Houghton Mifflin, 1978): pp. 498–533.

Lesnick, Daniel R., "Insults and threats in medieval Todi," *Journal of Medieval History*, vol. 17, no. 1 (March 1991): pp. 71–91.

Miller, Marion S., "Wagnerism, Wagnerians, and Italian Identity," in Large and Weber (1984): pp. 167–197.

Mosse, George, "Beauty Without Sensuality," in Barron (1991): pp. 25–31.

Parker, Andrew, "Unthinking Sex: Marx, Engels, and the Scene of Writing," *Social Text*, 29, vol. 9, no. 4 (1991): pp. 28–46.

Pivato, Stefano, *"Ginnastica e risorgimento: alle origini del rapporto sport/nazionalismo*; *Ricerche storiche*, vol. XIX, no. 2 (May 1989): pp. 249–280.

Pomata, Gianna, "Unwed Mothers in the Late Nineteenth and Early Twentieth Centuries: Clinical Histories and Life Histories," in Muir and Ruggiero (1991): pp. 159–204.

Remafredi, Gary, and James A. Farrow and Robert W. Deisher, "Risk Factors for Attempted Suicide in Gay and Bisexual Youth," *Pediatrics*, vol. 87, no. 6 (June 1991): pp. 869–75.

Romanelli, Raffaele, "Political Debate, Social History, and the Italian Borghesia: Changing Perspectives in Historical Research," *Journal of Modern History*, vol. 63, no. 4 (Dec. 1991): pp. 717–39.

Rubin, Gayle, "Thinking Sex: Notes for a Radical Theory of the Politics of Sexuality," in Vance (1984): pp. 267–319.

Schwarzenberg, Claudio, *"Fra storia urbana e storia giuridica: la capitale nell'età giolittiana,"* in Mola (1979): pp. 251–62.

Serra, Maurizio, *"Al di là della decadenza: Marinetti, la grande guerra e la rivolta futurista,"* *Storia contemporanea*, XXII, no. 6 (Dec. 1991): pp. 975–1037.

Staderini, Alessandra, *"L'interventismo romano, 1914-1915,"* *Storia contemporanea*, vol. XXII, no. .2 (April 1991): pp. 257–304.
Steinberg, Jonathon, "The Historian and the *Questione della Lingua*," in Burke and Porter (1987): pp. 198–209.

Vigezzi, Brunello, "Italian Socialism and the First World War," *Journal of Italian History*, vol. 2, no. 2 (Autumn 1979): pp. 232–56.

Vitale, Vincenzo, *L'anti giuridicità 'strutturale' del suicidio*, in D'Agostino (1984): pp. 121-45.

Vivarelli, Roberto, "Interpretations of the Origins of Fascism," *Journal of Modern History*, vol. 63, no. 1 (March 1991): pp. 29–43.

Warner, Michael, "Fear of a Queer Planet," *Social Text*, 29, vol. 9, no. 4 (1991): pp. 3–17.

Zanolla, Flaviano, "Mothers-in-law, Daughters-in-law, and Sisters-in-law at the Beginning of the Twentieth Century in P. of Friuli," in Muir and Ruggero (1990): pp. 177–99.

Index

Studies in Modern European History

The monographs in this series focus upon aspects of the political, social, economic, cultural, and religious history of Europe from the Renaissance to the present. Emphasis is placed on the states of Western Europe, especially Great Britain, France, Italy, and Germany. While some of the volumes treat internal developments, others deal with movements such as liberalism, socialism, and industrialization, which transcend a particular country.

The series editor is:

Frank J. Coppa
Director, Doctor of Arts Program
in Modern World History
Department of History
St. John's University
Jamaica, New York 11439

To order other books in this series, please contact our Customer Service Department:

(800) 770-LANG (within the U.S.)
(212) 647-7706 (outside the U.S.)
(212) 647-7707 FAX

or browse online by series at:
WWW.PETERLANGUSA.COM